Ubiratan Silva da Silva

# The role and skills of the designer in IT teams

Ubiratan Silva da Silva

# The role and skills of the designer in IT teams

## A case study

ScienciaScripts

**Imprint**

Any brand names and product names mentioned in this book are subject to trademark, brand or patent protection and are trademarks or registered trademarks of their respective holders. The use of brand names, product names, common names, trade names, product descriptions etc. even without a particular marking in this work is in no way to be construed to mean that such names may be regarded as unrestricted in respect of trademark and brand protection legislation and could thus be used by anyone.

Cover image: www.ingimage.com

This book is a translation from the original published under ISBN 978-613-9-62683-0.

Publisher:
Sciencia Scripts
is a trademark of
Dodo Books Indian Ocean Ltd. and OmniScriptum S.R.L publishing group

120 High Road, East Finchley, London, N2 9ED, United Kingdom
Str. Armeneasca 28/1, office 1, Chisinau MD-2012, Republic of Moldova, Europe
Printed at: see last page
ISBN: 978-620-7-74906-5

# SUMMARY

I dedicate it to my father Odilon da Silva and my mother Nelly Silva da Silva and to my children Ulisses and Yasmin for giving me life.

# ACKNOWLEDGMENTS

To God, the basis of everything I believe in.

Especially to my father Odilon da Silva (in memorian) who taught me the value of education as a tool for transforming human beings and values such as honesty and responsibility. To my mother Nelly Silva da Silva who always believed in her son's potential. My sister Elza Dolores da Silva who planted a love of art in my heart and soul and discovered my vocation for design. To Luna Clara Fernandez de Cândido, my companion who debated work issues with me, revised my writing and put up with my moods during this period of intense struggle with love and understanding.

To my advisor Professor Dr. Guilherme Correa Meyer who has the humility of the greats, knowledge, objectivity and more than guiding me, he motivated me to get to the end of the research like a friend. To the fantastic professors I met when I decided to take the challenging master's course, especially Professor Dr. Celso Scaletsky for renewing my admiration for design and for being a designer and for his permanent interest in evolving and researching, Professor Dr. Felipe Campelo Xavier for his contributions to the work and his permanent and fraternal dialogue, Professor Dr. Gustavo Borba for teaching me how to design. Gustavo Borba for teaching the most interesting and fun classes on innovation, even on Saturday mornings, and for spontaneously and innovatively creating the class logo, the famous star, Professor Dr. Leandro Tonetto with his talent for design and his constant interest in evolution and research. Leandro Tonetto who, with his talent, vast knowledge and good humor, turns scientific methodology classes into unforgettable moments, Professor Dr. Carlo Franzatto for his intelligent discussions in hybrid languages and also the esteemed professors Professor Dr. Karine Freire and Professor Dr. Ione Betz for their humility and immense knowledge.

To the special colleagues I met in the best Master's in Design class of all time, Juliana Wolfarth for her invaluable support at various times, Fernanda Ferreti, Isabel Cris D'avilla, companions in ideas and spirit, Gustavo Reis, an example of dedication and a partner in guitar and magazines, Débora Lemos, Caco Arnt, Raul Merch, Pedro Piantà, Adriana Galli Velho, Monica Greggianin Arlete Fante, Viviane Peçaibes (I'm your fan), Kaori Ishirara and her beautiful family, Clarissa Brinkmann and her beautiful family, Ane Rose, Tobias Camargo (hitchhiking partner), Aline Von Ahnt, Viviane Almada, Ederson Locatelli, Priscila Westphal for always being so kind and motivating, Adriano Debus, Marina Rambo, Silvio Vasconcellos, Marcelo Halpern, Luciane Candido, Sandra Heck, Livia Menezes and Marcelo Turchetti. I made a point of mentioning all my esteemed colleagues and thanking them for the opportunity to meet and get to know them. I don't think I've forgotten anyone, and I apologize if I have.

My bosses and coworkers Jeanine Heller and Lucienne Panno for their invaluable support in carrying out the research and my colleagues Alessandra Nunes, Heli Meurer, Marcos Falavenna and Eunice Alves for their constant motivation. The company PROCERGS RS for its support and willingness to put itself forward as a field for scientific research and to understand the importance of design.

My bands Zumbira e os Palmares and Grass Effect, who understood and supported the academic moment of their vocalist, guitarist and composer.

To my children Ulisses and Yasmin, everything I do is for you.

"Life can only be re-invented."

(Cecilia Meireles)

# SUMMARY

Contemporary society is undergoing significant changes. A new fluid, dematerialized, interconnected and complex society is emerging. To meet the demands of this context, designers need to adapt to new times, new professional and social arrangements. In addition, they need to relate to others, working in an integrated way with different areas of knowledge in order to develop solutions that meet the complex demands of this new configuration of society. The aim of the research in this dissertation is to contribute to reflecting on the role and skills of the designer when integrating multidisciplinary teams in organizations. The methodological procedures chosen were focus group techniques applied to individual designers and semi-structured in-depth interviews, which will be applied to non-designer individuals who are members of multidisciplinary teams in a large public information technology company. At the end of this case study, the aim is to contribute to reflection on the role and competences of the designer working in teams and in permanent dialogue with other areas of knowledge.

**Keywords:** Role of the designer. Designer in teams. Designer competencies.

# 1. INTRODUCTION

Current studies in various areas of human knowledge indicate that profound transformations are taking place in society (MORIN, 1991; CASTELLS, 1999; LEVY, 2000, BRANZI, 2003). Previously, we lived in a reality marked by more stable concepts and practices, with established and somewhat predictable rules. This period has been characterized by many authors as the first modernity (BAUMAN, 2000; BRANZI, 2003), which lasts until around 1990, and by other authors it has been called the static scenario (LEVITT, 1990; MAURI, 1996) and also the modern project of society (MANZINI, 2004). It was a solid, defined world, characterized by the search for order, methods and the quantification of concepts. A concrete reality was sought and this obsessive search for order, stability and control was configured in the modern project for society.

As Manzini (2004) states, there were safe disciplinary containers in which any individual could position themselves, feeling well defined in their own professional identity (MANZINI, 2004). This stability was the result of a society made up of individuals who relied on linear behavior and who believed that this was the path to happiness for all people and the balance of society. This was the ideal of progress at the time and it guided industrial and technological development, as well as part of the ethics and aesthetics of much of 20th century thinking.

This configuration of modern, industrial society brought with it the emergence of previously underestimated activities and functions. As Michel Foucault states, the flow of control from the top down and the fact that the action of supervising became a highly skilled professional activity were traits that united a series of so-called modern inventions such as schools, military barracks, hospitals, psychiatric clinics, hospices, industrial parks and prisons. All these institutions of modern society were factories of order and, like all factories, they were places of deliberately structured activities in the quest to achieve previously established results: in this case, the aim was to restore certainty, eliminate any chance, make the behavior of the members themselves regular and predictable (FOUCAULT, 1969).

It is understood that the worldview that circumscribes the industrial revolution is one that exalts human reason and man's (working) ability to use it to shape the world in his own way, following the belief in a "progress" that would lead us to an egalitarian, fair, balanced and happy society.

This model of stability, the fruit of a capitalist and industrial society, has been questioned over time by artists, thinkers, philosophers and scientists. The so-called static scenario began to show itself as a fragile model incapable of responding to the increasingly complex demands of a society in transformation. The modernist model of a stable society destined for progress and the full happiness of all people is faced with profound transformations taking place in the most diverse areas of society and in the most diverse fields of knowledge. These transformations leave an entire generation that was brought up on this model (static and predictable) with the need to adapt to a new society, post-modern and post-industrial, whose essential characteristics are complexity, fluidity, dynamism and the need to deal with uncertainty and serious unforeseen problems.

As Mauri states:

> The dream of continuous, linear development has been shattered by emergencies that were not foreseen and which have proved essential to take into account, such as the reduction in the need for human labor and the widening gap between rich and poor, the degradation of the environment and the saturation of markets (Mauri, 1996).

In fact, as Andrea Branzi (2003) points out, the material world that surrounds us, the society in which we live today, is very different from what the modern movement had imagined. Instead of an industrial and rational order, today's metropolises present a highly diverse scenario, where opposing production logics and linguistic systems coexist without major contradictions (BRANZI, 2003).

We are currently living in a period of transition. We live in a complex, fluid, dynamic, globalized world, where one of the few certainties we can have is that things are constantly changing, connecting, disconnecting and reconnecting, in other words, permanently reorganizing themselves. As Manzini continues in his historical vision, in this fluid contemporary world, containers have been opened up and their walls are no longer protected, professional and disciplinary definitions and boundaries are dissolving and blending together (Manzini, 2004). As a result, everyone has to redefine themselves and their own baggage of references, skills, competences and capacities on a daily basis in order to integrate into the world and meet its complex demands.

In this new context, different realities coexist simultaneously and each individual, within their potential and competence, brings their own experiences of affection, concession, motivation, skills and abilities into their personal world. These experiences tend to connect with the plurality of values and meanings of the culture to which they belong, i.e. their social environment (ONO, 2006). This leads us to realize that social relationships are factors that need to be investigated, as they have a direct influence on the performance and development of a professional activity such as design.

Another consequence of this new configuration of society is dematerialization, the virtualization of relationships (LEVY, 1996 and 2000) and even deterritorialization (FOUCAULT, 1969; DELEUZE, 1972 and BAUDRILLARD, 1991), provided by the virtual world and its connections arising from this globalization and new technological means of communication, connection and computing.

The consequence of this development is the abolition of borders and physical distances between the components of society, between companies and organizations, between producers and consumers and an acceleration of relationships that are developing in greater numbers due to the possibilities provided by a network society (CASTELLS, 1999) and at much greater speed. This is a reflection of the fact that the new technologies and possibilities for connection and communication between individuals available today are significantly influencing the methods and techniques of the most diverse areas of knowledge and, consequently, the relationships that need to be established.

In this way, a new social dynamic has been established and some disciplines that were based on solid interpretations derived from a static scenario (predictable, exact data) have come into conflict with the reality of today's changing, dynamic and complex scenario, which is permeated with hybrid messages and codes that are subject to the most diverse interpretations and meanings. This globalization and abolition of borders makes society an intricate network of cultures, living together in relative harmony, but each culture with its own specificities and characteristics, seeking its own space, working to perpetuate itself as a genuine culture.

Seen as an activity whose function is to mediate dialectically between needs and objects, between production and consumption (MALDONADO, 1976), the activity of design has also been impacted by all the transformations that society has undergone. The process has developed, evolved and encountered new, unexpected and complex demands. Tools, methods and techniques have emerged over the years, affirming design as a key, even strategic discipline in the complex consumer society we live in today.

Given this dynamic context, there is a need to understand how design activity and the professional designer behave today, in contemporary times. In this way, it will be possible to really understand what their role is in society, in the social groups they belong to and what skills the current scenario demands for the performance of their activity, so that they can develop and evolve and even sustain themselves as professionals.

According to Mauri:

marketing, corporate culture, industry and design are mobilized in the discussion, in the search for interpretative keys and in the proposals for ways of solving problems in markets that are increasingly complex due to globalization, saturation and the speed of current transformations (MAURI, 1996).

Contemporaneity and its intrinsic complexity and dynamism make production and consumption two unknowns to be solved, which is why research into designers, their role and their skills requires a greater capacity for interpretation on the part of the researcher. It is necessary to complement research based solely on the technical aspects of obtaining statistical data from quantitative research with more qualitative visions that consider design as a phenomenon that involves different factors in order to happen in practice. A qualitative analysis is therefore needed that goes beyond the technical factors involved in the activity and considers the relationships necessary for the performance of the design activity, given that we are in a networked society and that nothing can be done absolutely alone or in isolation, practically everything and everyone is interconnected or has latent connection potential.

This complex set of changes that society is undergoing also influences the contexts of organizations and consequently the teams, social groups that are formed in organizations to meet the demands of this new configuration of society.

In the midst of so many changes, this study is particularly interested in investigating how the designer perceives himself and is perceived by the team and by the other members of the context in which his activity is inserted, in order to relate this perception to what actually happens in the practice of his activity. Therefore, the research problem on which this study will be developed is: what is the role of the designer when working in multidisciplinary teams and what would be the necessary skills perceived by designers and non-designers to work as a designer in these contexts?

By reflecting on this problem, the aim is to establish the congruences and discrepancies between what is expected of the designer and what happens in practice, in order to point out ways in which design can sustain itself and expand its work, and even seek out new knowledge and skills that are necessary to be developed along the way. It is therefore necessary to understand how the contemporary designer acts, reacts, adapts and evolves in the face of a changing society, strongly influenced by the development of technology and increasing complexity.

The literature on design is rich in studies of designers who carried out their creative activity alone or in isolation, independently, almost like artists or genius inventors who developed their own methods and techniques for making artifacts, which shaped their work process (SIMON, 1981; SCHON, 1983).

Today, it is clear that as well as working in these two previous contexts, designers also work in larger, more heterogeneous teams, made up of professional designers and non-designers from the most diverse areas of knowledge, working in a transversal and integrated manner to develop more complex solutions.

As Flaviano Celaschi states:

> The designer has become a key player in the world of production and consumption, whose knowledge is typically multidisciplinary because of the way he or she thinks about the product itself, because he or she is at the center of the relationship between consumption and production, because of the need to understand the preferences and dynamics of the value network and, above all, because his or her actions must be able to modify or confer new values on products through his or her design interventions. Designers also tend to promote the synthesis of theoretical concepts and transfer them as a formal response to satisfaction, desire or need (Celaschi, 2000).

It can thus be seen that design relates to the tangible and the intangible, necessarily with product/service systems that involve its conception and consumption, and it is therefore necessary to take a systemic view of its action and integration into society.

The general aim of this research is to reflect on the role and skills of the designer in a collective environment, more specifically in multidisciplinary teams.

Therefore, it is understood that a study of this type can contribute to a more up-to-date analysis of the context of contemporary culture in which the designer is inserted, revealing technical aspects about his creative systems and also social aspects involved in the relationships that he, as a designer and multidisciplinary professional, needs to establish in order to practice his activity.

In this context, the aim is to observe the designer not only in terms of the technical and procedural aspects of their activity, such as methods, techniques, tools and skills, which have already been widely studied in the design literature, but also in terms of the social aspects, the relationships that involve their integration with teams, other designers and non-designers, and the factors of organizational culture that influence their work.

All these aspects need to be taken into account, as they directly influence the designer's practice and the impact of this influence varies according to the experience of each designer and their skills in solving the problems that arise. Experience is understood here as the sum of the knowledge acquired formally, in schools and technical courses (training and further training), undergraduate courses, postgraduate courses and the knowledge accumulated in real cases, where formal knowledge is practiced in order to solve the real problems presented to the designer throughout their professional career.

What motivated me as a researcher is the fact that, for more than 15 years, I worked as a graphic designer and web designer in this organization and noticed many transformations taking place in the practice of my activity. During this time I had the opportunity to work in different contexts, sharing or not sharing my creative process with designers and non-designers, which allowed me to observe different ways of working. I have followed the development of various technologies, methods and techniques, as well as the emergence of tools and software that have appeared throughout this period, and which have forced me to constantly seek to update my knowledge and adapt in order to continue performing my activity as a designer in a successful way. This diversity of situations and contexts, directly influenced by the impact of new technologies and a new configuration of society, has instigated me to seek a better understanding of the aspects that most influence the practice of the contemporary designer in order to try to develop ways of adapting to these transformations.

Aspects that are often not purely technical, since mastering the technique is not enough to enter the job market and establish yourself as a prosperous professional. In performing my job, relationships with other people have always been fundamental and intrinsic to the activity and just as important, if not more so, than mastering techniques and methods.

In this way, understanding how this transformation in the designer's process happens, what technical and social factors influence the performance of his activity in contemporary times, as well as now being an object of study and research for me, also means deepening my knowledge of a reality with which I have been familiar for more than 15 years working in the company that will be observed.

In order to carry out this study, which is classified as qualitative, exploratory and based on a case study, and because it considers two different audiences whose views need to be taken into account in order to get a broader idea of the subject, it was decided to use techniques that were appropriate to the objectives and audiences. Thus, for designers, the chosen technique will be the focus group, so that a group conversation between professionals from the same class can be used to reliably and spontaneously discuss the issues that influence the theme of the role and competencies of the designer.

In order to understand the perception of non-designers about the role and performance of the designer in the teams they are part of, the research technique chosen will be semi-structured in-depth interviews, since there is a need to keep the conversation on a central theme that will be developed through a script of questions related to the theme and objectives of the research.

Content analysis will be applied to the transcribed content of the two techniques (focus group and semi-structured in-depth interviews). This content analysis will have as its guiding principles the analysis of some factors related to aspects that should be considered for a correct understanding of the role and competencies of the designer when working in these teams and organizations. The observation of these aspects will serve as a starting point for organizing the analysis of the data, in order to focus the observation on factors that relate to the role of the designer and the skills needed to perform this role, specifically when working in multidisciplinary teams.

The specific objectives of this research are thus met:

•	To identify DESIGNERS' perceptions of the role and competencies of the designer working in multidisciplinary teams;

•	To identify the perceptions of NON-DESIGNERS about the role and competencies of the designer working in multidisciplinary teams;

•	To establish a synthetic set of competencies for working as a designer in multidisciplinary teams, based on a parallel between the two visions;

•	To identify the difficulties encountered by designers in carrying out their work in multidisciplinary teams.

•	Identify how designers and non-designers perceive the influence of organizational culture on the role and performance of designers in multidisciplinary teams;

•	Identify aspects related to the nature (type) of the transformation that occurs with the role of the designer in an organization/company and in teams.

Thus, by achieving the specific objectives, it will be possible to reflect on the role and skills of the designer working in these contexts, specifically working in multidisciplinary teams, which is the general objective of this study.

The organization chosen for the application of this research, i.e. the case to be studied, is PROCERGS, a large public information technology company. It was chosen because its staff includes designers of varying levels of experience and non-designers, who need to establish relationships and exchange knowledge for the success of the solutions they seek to develop. This company was also chosen because it represents a typical example of a contemporary organization, involved in developing solutions to current problems and which, therefore, needs to be multidisciplinary and encompass a variety of integrated knowledge in order to compose the complex solutions required of it.

This organization, whose mission is to provide information and communication technology solutions to increase the efficiency and transparency of public service and bring government and citizens closer together, has been in existence for over 40 years, having been founded in 1972. About 20 years ago, with the advent of the Internet and its graphical interface, the World Wide Web, it realized that the inclusion of designers would be important for improving its solutions. These were information technology solutions, which involved creating interfaces between computerized services provided by the government and the citizen.

It was believed in this organization that by applying the designers' specific technical knowledge, the performance of the solutions could be improved, even optimized. The designer's role and responsibility would then be to worry about aesthetic aspects (relating to the shape of the solution), which would make the use of the solution more pleasant, but above all, he or she would have to worry about the usability of the solution, to make it easier for the end user to learn and use it in practice, in other words, the design of such interfaces should be *user-centered design*. This approach led the organization studied to start admitting designers to its public tenders from 1997 onwards and since then it has had designers integrated into the development teams of its solutions.

In this environment, designers are part of multidisciplinary teams developing information technology solutions and sometimes carry out their creative process in isolation, sometimes collaboratively (sharing the creative design process), but always integrated with other professionals from other areas of knowledge such as programmers, systems analysts, business analysts, managers, clients and end users of the solution.

Having presented the context of complexity and the interconnected society, the transformations that society and its organizations are undergoing and the social groups that make it up, companies and teams, the research problem, the researcher's motivations, the research objectives, the field of observation, the individuals and the research method and techniques, the aim is to construct a research project that will address the following topics:

Firstly, a theoretical framework that will cover studies on the role and competences of the designer in the literature, from the definition of the term design, through the evaluation of the role of the designer in organizations, changes in roles in the design process, concepts of competence, concepts of organizational culture, concepts of teams and multidisciplinarity and finally concepts of human-centered design (HCD), *user-centered* design (UCD) and interaction design related to the nature of the solutions that the designer develops in the company studied. After the theoretical framework, the method used and the techniques used to investigate and analyze the information will be presented. After the method, the results of the research deemed most important in relation to the objectives and subject of the study will be presented. This will be followed by a discussion in which the information collected will be interpreted in the light of the concepts raised in the theoretical framework and, finally, the researcher's final comments on the research carried out.

In this way, the main contribution of this research is to provide qualitative support through the views of professionals in these environments for a broad reflection on the role of the designer in the social contexts in which they operate in contemporary society, as well as a survey of the competencies required, expected and practiced in the performance of this role.

## 1.1 DEFINING THE TOPIC OR PROBLEM

To identify the role(s) of the designer working in multidisciplinary teams and the competencies required to perform these role(s), based on an exploratory case study in a public information technology company that will consider the views of designers and non-designers who work as part of the teams.

## 1.2  BOUNDARIES OF THE WORK

This qualitative and exploratory research based on a case study is interested in reflecting on the role of the designer in multidisciplinary teams, i.e. when integrated with professionals from other areas of knowledge, and also on what skills are needed to work as a designer in this context, as perceived and expected by designers and non-designers. What is of interest here are the technical and non-technical skills that enable design professionals to work in these contexts and fulfill their role(s).

## 1.3  OBJECTIVES

The objectives are divided into general and specific.

### 1.3.1 General Objective

Reflect on the role and skills of the designer working in multidisciplinary teams

**1.3.2 Specific Objectives**

a)     to identify DESIGNERS' perceptions of the role and competencies of the designer working in multidisciplinary teams;

b)     to identify the perceptions of NON-DESIGNERS about the role and competencies of the designer working in multidisciplinary teams;

c)     to establish a summary set of competencies for working as a designer in multidisciplinary teams, based on a parallel between the two visions;

d)     to identify difficulties encountered by designers in carrying out their work in multidisciplinary teams;

e)     to identify how the influence of organizational culture on the role and performance of designers in multidisciplinary teams is perceived by designers and non-designers;

f)     identify aspects related to the nature (type) of the transformation that occurs with the role of the designer in an organization/company and in teams.

## 1.4 BACKGROUND

This research is interested in understanding the impact of the transformations that contemporary society is undergoing on design activity. Therefore, it was considered important to analyze the designer acting in the new contexts that arise in this new complex and interconnected society. To do this, a typical company of today was chosen, such as information technology companies, and more specifically in multidisciplinary teams, where the designer needs to understand the set of technical and non-technical skills required to act as such.

This opportunity arose because the researcher was an employee of the company, which has designers working in multidisciplinary teams developing software (websites and internet service systems), and was close to the context, with access to the company's designers and non-designers.

# 2. THEORETICAL FRAMEWORK

In order to establish the theoretical framework for this research into the role and competencies of the contemporary designer in multidisciplinary teams, it was decided to first present concepts that relate directly to this topic.

Firstly, we need to address the difficult and ambiguous nature of the term design and the evolution of this concept over time. Then we intend to look at the role of design and the designer in organizations, as presented by important authors on the subject, and the changes that this role has undergone with the transformations that society has undergone, so that at the end of the research it will be possible to establish a comparison between the theory and the practice observed in the field. After studying the role of the designer, the question of competences will be addressed, seeking to establish a useful and consistent definition for this research that conceptualizes competence in a general sense and in the specific sense of the designer's competences, since it is believed that it is from the practical mobilization of competences that the designer plays his role in society.

As this is a study focused on the aspects involved in the designer's work in a group (multidisciplinary teams), after addressing competencies, definitions of multidisciplinarity and organizational culture will be presented, so that we arrive at the social group of teams, where the designer will be observed and invited to construct information about their role and competencies.

Based on this theoretical discussion confronted with the findings of the observation and interviews, it is believed that a significant contribution can be made to understanding the skills that are mobilized by designers so that they can play their role in the collective spheres of contemporary society.

2.1 THE DEFINITION OF THE TERM DESIGN

First of all, we need to discuss the definitions of the term design. It's a broad term, full of different meanings and ambiguities that make it difficult to understand and reach a consensus on its definition.

Design has its earliest etymological origins in Latin, linked to the verb *designare,* which is used both to designate and to draw (CARDOSO, 2013). The word design has its primary origin in the English language, which contains an ambiguity. It has an abstract element in that the term refers to the idea of planning, design and intention. Therefore, its use is linked to intellectual concepts and, on the other hand, to a concrete element, be it related to the identification of the term with an idea of configuration, arrangement or structure.

The records of the use of the word design in this sense, according to Martins (2007), are related to English-speaking countries, more precisely during the Industrial Revolution, which gave rise to new uses corresponding to new productive activities, such as the act of planning and designing. In this context, it became increasingly necessary to differentiate the act of drawing (to draw) from the act of planning, projecting, designating, schematizing (to design).

In 1957, ICSID, the International Council of Societies of Industrial Design, was founded, which defined the guidelines for design (industrial design) in the second half of the 20th century. These guidelines aimed to exclude the idea of the designer having an artistic character or being involved in the purely aesthetic and personal field and emphasized technical knowledge.

In 1958, this council presented a definition of design, more specifically of the designer, which read as follows:

"Designing the form means coordinating, integrating and articulating all those factors that, in one way or another, participate in the constitutive process of the product's form (...) This refers both to factors relating to the use, enjoyment and individual or social consumption of the product (functional, symbolic or cultural factors) and to those relating to its production (technical-economic, technical-constructive, technical-systematic, technical-productive and technical-distributive factors)" (ICSID, 1958).

In the definition made a year later, in 1959, ICSID presented a few more attributes of the activity:

"The industrial designer is someone qualified by training, technical knowledge, experience and visual sensitivity to determine materials, mechanisms, shapes, colors, finishes and decorations of objects produced in quantity by industrial processes." (ICSID, 1959).

It can be seen that these definitions were more concerned with defining who the design professional was and what their attributions were within an industrial context, i.e. designers had to be concerned not only with aesthetic-formal aspects, but also with commercial aspects and the large-scale production of their artifacts. Furthermore, the industrial designer was someone who: "was concerned with the form of the artifacts, with an a priori idea about the aesthetic-functional value of the form and, who carried out a design activity, whose motivations, are situated apart from and precede the constitutive process of the form itself" (ICSID, 1959).

In 1961, Tomâs Maldonado criticized this definition and broadened its concept. According to Maldonado (1961):

> Designing the form means coordinating, integrating and articulating all those factors that in some way participate in the constitutive process of the product's form". This refers precisely to factors relating to the use, enjoyment and individual or social consumption of the product (functional, symbolic or cultural factors) as well as those relating to its production (technical-systematic, technical-productive and technical-distributive factors) (MALDONADO, 1961).

From this point of view, design began to be seen within a context where various factors and aspects were related, although the focus was still on the product produced or designed.

ICSID currently defines design as:

> "A creative activity whose aim is to establish the qualities of objects, processes, services and their systems in all life cycles." Therefore, design is the central factor in the innovative humanization of technologies and the crucial factor in cultural and economic exchange. One of the tasks of design is to discover and evaluate structural, organizational, functional and economic relationships in order to strengthen global sustainability and environmental protection (global ethics), provide benefits and freedom for the entire human community, individual and collective, end users, producers and market players (social ethics), support cultural diversity, despite the globalization of the world (cultural ethics) by generating products, services and systems that have expressive forms (semiology) and are coherent with the aesthetics of their own complexity. Design refers to products, services and systems conceived with the tools, organization and logic introduced by industrialization (ICSID, 2014).

The most up-to-date ICSID definition no longer simply refers to the conception of a product and its formal and aesthetic aspects. The definition of design has been expanded, going beyond the product and involving the services related to this product, requiring a systemic vision, given the wide range of connections and relationships that design needs to establish in order to develop as a professional activity in contemporary society.

In summary, it is clear from the above definitions how difficult it is to conceptualize the activity of design, as well as how it has changed over time, a change that has been permanently influenced by various factors.

## 2.2 THE ROLE OF DESIGN AND DESIGNERS IN ORGANIZATIONS

According to the strategic design approach, the term designer refers to an individual who practices an intellectual, systemic profession with social and environmental responsibility, and not simply a business or a service for companies (MANZINI, VEZZOLI, 2002). In this way, this professional must act as a mediator who manages to mediate production and consumption relationships, always seeking to reconcile the aesthetic-formal issue with the function of the product/service systems he designs.

The author Meroni (2008) complements this view by stating that designers are professionals with particular skills, who become part of the community they are collaborating with, helping it professionally to make strategic decisions and design its future. The dynamics of design, thought of from the perspective of sustainability, are initiatives that have the capacity to articulate individual interests with social and environmental interests, which, in the search for concrete solutions, reinforce the social fabric (MERONI, 2008).

In the words of Flaviano Celaschi (2000):

> The designer has become a key player in the world of production and consumption, whose knowledge is typically multidisciplinary because of the way he or she thinks about the product itself, because he or she is at the center of the relationship between consumption and production, because of the need to understand the preferences and dynamics of the value network and, above all, because his or her actions must be able to modify or confer new values on products through his or her design interventions. Designers also tend to promote the synthesis of theoretical concepts and transfer them as a formal response to satisfaction, desire or need (CELASCHI, 2000).

Given this scenario, design, from a systemic and interdisciplinary viewpoint, has increasingly taken on the strategic role of mediator between consumption and production and facilitator in the generation and management of knowledge in organizations. It is a strategic tool both in recognizing and translating cultural values and signs to generate symbolic and cultural meaning for products, services and systems, and in investigating and bringing together different worlds and lifestyles. As such, design professionals can act as mediators between production and consumption and between cultures. Mediated in the sense used by Gilberto Velho, who defines the term as:

> The role played by individuals who are interpreters and move between different social segments and domains (...). Although they originally belong to a specific group, neighborhood or moral region, they develop the talent and ability to mediate between different worlds (VELHO, 2001).

These characteristics are strongly evident in design activities that involve different agents in the context in which they intervene. These activities, which in some cases are called codesign activities, share the assumption that when these agents are actively involved in the process of finding solutions to their desires, the results tend to be efficient, long-lasting and satisfactory (MANZINI, 2008).

According to Zurlo (2010) and in line with the strategic design approach, the designer who acts according to this perspective operates in collective spheres, supports strategic action thanks to their own capabilities, generates effects of meaning, which is the dimension of value for someone, and materializes this result in product/service systems that are the tangible representations of the organization's strategy (ZURLO, 2010). Inserting design as a strategic activity in the organizational culture represents a significant change in the organization's management and processes. To bring about this change in organizational culture, strategic design relies on the capabilities defined by Francesco Zurlo as *design capabilities*:

-       the ability to see, understood as the ability to read contexts and systems in an oriented way;

-       The ability to foresee, understood as the ability to critically anticipate the future and uncertainties;

-       The ability to see, understood as the ability to visualize future scenarios. (ZURLO, 2010).

Based on these skills or competencies, (strategic) design needs to be able to conduct an orchestra made up of different disciplines so that at the end of the process there is a new and original musical solution (product/service system).

Thus, from this systemic and interdisciplinary viewpoint, design has increasingly taken on the strategic role of mediator and facilitator in the generation and management of knowledge in organizations. Given the communication and connection resources that exist today, conditions that have transformed society into a huge network made up of other networks and the most diverse actors, strategic design presents itself as a methodological alternative for organizing and producing for people with converging objectives who work in these networks and in the organizations that make them up.

Strategic design as a discipline and activity, according to Zurlo (2010), operates in collective spheres, supports strategic action thanks to its own capabilities, generates effects of meaning, which is the dimension of value for someone, concretizing this result in product/service systems that are the tangible representations of the organization's strategy (ZURLO, 2010). As the author states:

"Strategic design is therefore a complex phenomenon that is confronted with complex phenomena: trying to interpret it means not giving in to simplifying intentions. The aim, therefore, is not so much to look for a single reading key, but to take in, through phenomenology, the wealth of expressions and, for our purposes, some recurring characters. These include: its situated dimension (the dependence on the circumstances of the action); the ability to enable, with one's own skills and competences, a dialogical process between more actors (multidisciplinarity); the requirement to satisfy different needs while obtaining (recognized) results of value" (ZURLO, 2004).

For Zurlo (2004), the collective sphere in which strategic design operates is an organized structure, often like a company. Generally, within this organized structure, there is already a base of values, knowledge and methodologies and techniques that indicate to itself and to others the environment, the reason and the process, factors that characterize the action as an organized group in society (MINTZBERG, 1994). This basis is referred to in strategic planning literature as a model. This model ends up characterizing the entire philosophy of the organization and its actions in the market and in society.

According to Zurlo (2004), the model is capable of indicating a direction and also of providing cohesion within a structure. The entire organization and its leaders adapt their behaviour in accordance with this basic orientation. Making this model clear and explicit, as well as contributing to the definition of the organization's identity is, for Zurlo, the first practical area of action for strategic design and requires a way of operating similar to communication and corporate image design.

According to the strategic design approach, the designer must operate taking into account other aspects that influence the behavior and motivation of individuals. These are cultural and social aspects linked to material and immaterial elements, symbols and specific rituals that are characteristic of all human activity and which are embodied in the routine and style that characterizes the organization (MINTZBERG, 1994). As such, the model can be considered to be a reflection of an organization's identity, resulting from the sum and negotiation of the identities of its founders and members, as well as a complex system of actors who are configured as stakeholders (Stanford's definition, 1963). This is why the organization is able to achieve the things it sets out to do as a group, a collective sphere.

Strategic design is therefore characterized by the mobilization of design skills and competences in order to shape an organization's strategy. To achieve this goal, it uses a systemic vision that needs to consider the various factors and actors involved and interrelated that make up the systems and networks of today's society. In this way, it develops product-service systems, i.e. coherent sets of activities and means of communication (product, service, communication) from which the company or organization builds its own identity and thus positions itself in the market. In this systemic vision, relationships gain greater emphasis and can determine the success or failure of the design process and the product-service system that is produced through this process.

As such, the role of the designer, according to the strategic design approach, shifts within an organization. They are no longer simply an operational resource responsible for the formal and aesthetic aspects of a product or service, but also an influencer and definer of an organization's model, identity and, consequently, strategy in the market and in society.

For Manzini (2008), the shift in focus from physical products to an integrated system of goods and services aims to offer solutions to consumers. It is an innovation strategy in which the focus of a company's business migrates from designing (and marketing) physical products to designing (and marketing) a system of goods and services that work together to satisfy a specific customer demand. However, as Meroni states, products and services have always been connected, although this connection has often been ephemeral, casual and left to the individual initiative of those who sell or purchase a product (MERONI, 2008).

The designer, according to the strategic design approach, needs to establish relationships with a wide range of professions and areas of knowledge through the practice of their *skills*, connecting and integrating into collective processes for developing product-service systems. It therefore needs to perceive society as a larger system (systemic vision), made up of interconnected subsystems, larger and smaller networks, connected or in the process of connection and disconnection, diverse actors, diverse and connected social and cultural situations and contexts.

Other studies that seek to broaden the scope of the designer's work from a strategic perspective contribute to understanding this activity within organizations by defining appropriate roles and competencies for this activity.

According to Mozota (2003), an author in the field of design management, design plays a primarily instrumental role in business processes. The author presents design as an activity that has four levels of influence on the organization: as a differentiator, as an integrator, as a transformer and as good business for society (MOZOTA, 2003). According to the author, these four forces of design interact directly with management and contribute to improving the company's results in terms of the market, talent, processes and, consequently, finances. In this way, there is scope for design as a discipline to move from an operational level to a strategic level in company structures (MOZOTA, 2003).

According to Katheryne Best (2006), design is closely linked to the way in which society, the environment and business interact, and as a result the organization is beginning to understand design more and more as a strategic factor to be managed in the organization (BEST, 2006). Faced with so many relationships, the discipline of strategic design, with its systemic vision that focuses on relationships, plays an important role in the management of the organization and is directly related to its strategy.

Still on the subject of the role of design and the designer, it is important to present more recent concepts on the subject in the book Design for a Complex World by Rafael Cardoso (CARDOSO, 2013). In this book, which seeks to make a historical survey of the role of the designer over time, what have been considered the most important attributes of design activity are presented.

In the first place, and presented as the most important attribute, the author suggests that it is the designer's capacity for systemic thinking. In this sense, the author presents this attribute as the designer's great differential and contribution to solving the demands of the complex world (CARDOSO, 2013). This statement indicates that in order to act as a designer in today's world (complex world), you need a special ability to consider problems in an integrated way, where each part, each element and their relationship with each other must be considered. This idea goes hand in hand with the attribute of multidisciplinarity presented earlier by Celaschi (CELASCHI, 2000), as a characteristic of the contemporary designer, because in order to achieve systemic thinking, connections between different types of knowledge are necessary, and in this sense few activities are as prepared for this task as design.

The second attribute cited by Cardoso as typical of good design is inventiveness of language, which is the ability to create, understand, manipulate and combine different languages that are generally visual and/or plastic. This statement brings design closer to activities such as arts and crafts. However, as the same author states, the creative and artistic side of design was systematically underestimated throughout the 20th century, combated by an ideology that aimed to establish design methodology on a supposedly scientific basis, which distances design from the plastic arts and from

(CARDOSO, 2013). If we consider art to be a means of accessing the unknown, as well as science and philosophy, it is possible to understand design as more related to art than to the latter two areas, since design is a field that aims to materialize ideas and shares with art, architecture and engineering the purpose of shaping forms, spaces and defining relationships of meaning, usually of a visual and tactile nature.

The third attribute of design presented arises from what would be the synthesis of the meaning of terms such as efficiency, elegance, caprice, mastery, virtuosity. This attribute is defined by Glberto Paim as the term craftsmanship, a neologism suggested to translate the English word craftsmanship (PAIM, 2008 apud CARDOSO 2013). *Craftsmanship is* understood as a high degree of attention to detail and care in the execution of the task, stemming from a peculiar sense of pride in the work, the pleasure of doing it well. This attribute, although present in other activities, seems to be evident in the design activity and in the best projects. This attribute is also linked to the idea of suitability for purpose, i.e. the idea that appearance/form can be expressive of a certain economy of means and elegance of solutions (CARDOSO, 2013).

The discussion of the attributes presented by Cardoso (2013) help to understand the relationship between design and art and can be verified or not in the discussion chapter of this dissertation, where these concepts will be confronted with the results of the field trip.

2.3 CHANGING ROLES IN THE DESIGN PROCESS

The advance of technology within this society has meant that the roles in the design process of a product or service have changed, making it increasingly difficult to define the boundaries between the client, the designer and the end user.

This situation allows for a twofold view of the situation. On the one hand, there is a strategic need to include the end user in the early stages of the design process in order to meet the increasingly complex demands of our society and even to help redefine design problems, and on the other hand, there is a unique opportunity to gather real insights from situations of practical use of the tool which, when considered in the design phase, become suppliers of ideas and insights to generate incremental innovations, improvements and adaptations for its users.

For such a situation to become truly productive, the user no longer needs to be just the direction of the solution, the channel for the message, the *output*. The user needs to participate in the design process in a more effective and concrete way, including in the initial phases of the project, and in the permanent definition and redefinition of the design problem, also participating in the process parallel to the project, sometimes called metaproject or metadesign (DE MORAES, 2010), where subsidies are sought for the design phase of the solution.

The traditional concept of the design process admits three roles: the user who consumes the product, who will buy it and use it on a daily basis, the designer who conceives the product, creates, designs and executes it in order to end up with an artifact (product or service interface), and the client who usually manufactures, distributes and markets the product, as illustrated in figure 1 (STAPPERS, VISSER, and KISTEMAKER, 2011).

Figura 1 - Traditional view of the design process

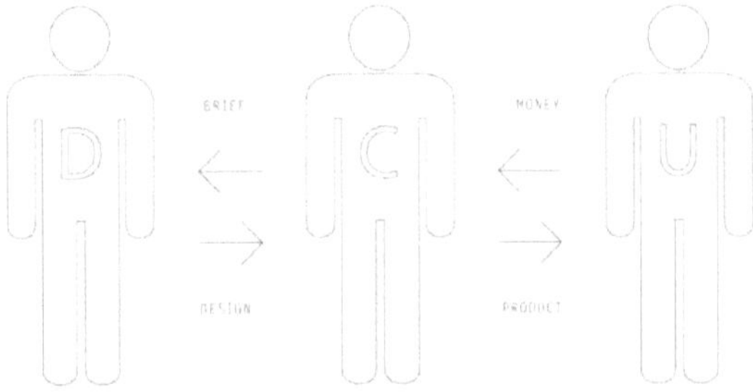


Source: Stappers, Visser and Kistemaker (2011).

With the advance of technology, this division into three levels has made it significantly more difficult to define the boundaries between one role and another, and in many fields these roles are intertwined. One area where this happens more intensely is in the development of IT services for companies and citizens (government) usually interfaced by a machine, a computer, a piece of software, in the case of this research an online public services website.

The people who control the design process are seeing that the user can be a source of valuable information, not just a channel for directing output (STAPPERS, VISSER, and KISTEMAKER, 2011).

In this sense, the role of the designer is also changing. There needs to be a link of empathy between the end user and the designer, so that the designer can put themselves in the user's shoes when designing solutions, and vice versa. This is what could be defined as a user-centered-design approach (SANDERS and STAPPERS, 2003).

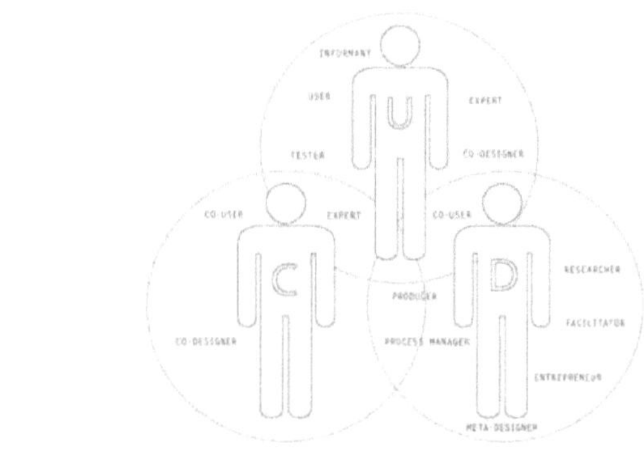


Source: Stappers, Visser and Kistemaker (2011).

## 2.4 COMPETENCIES

The term "competence" is used both in common parlance and in the professional and academic environments of psychologists, educators and others. It is usually used to characterize attributes of human individuals, in terms of a kind of potential. As defined by Carrol (1958):

> Competence is the actual power to perform a physical or mental activity or act, which is achieved through training and education (CARROL, 1958).

Competences or abilities (German Fahigkeiten, English abilities) in psychology are the personality traits that enable an individual to achieve a certain accomplishment or performance. Ability should not, however, be confused with performance itself, which can vary according to motivation (ASENDORPF, 2004).

A person's skills can be organized into a hierarchy, with more general and more specific skills. Depending on the interest of the study, numerous such hierarchies can be constructed, whether for musical, sporting, literary, intellectual or social skills, for example.

Many studies in the design literature deal with the competencies or skills needed by the designer to carry out his or her professional activity, so competencies are an important issue when investigating the role of the contemporary designer, as it is through them that the designer will play his or her role.

Another definition that contributes to a better understanding of the word competence for the purposes of this research comes from sociology and is proposed by Zarifian (2001) as the capacity, ability or aptitude of human beings to solve problems. It consists of a practical understanding of certain situations and is based on knowledge acquired by the professional. This knowledge is applied in practice and transformed as the diversity of situations increases (ZARIFIAN, 2001).

Therefore, competence encompasses skill, but is not restricted to it, going beyond the mere technical question of the ability to operate. In the same way, competence encompasses attitude, but is not restricted to it, as it presupposes appropriate action and not just action. Competence presupposes action that adds value when faced with new situations. In this way we can understand the composition of the concept of competence, through objectively measurable criteria, as the proactive and simultaneous exercise of: (1) Knowing (qualification) - knowledge; (2) Knowing how to do (functional experience) - skill; (3) Knowing how to act (ability to obtain results) - attitude.

Knowledge in itself is associated with "knowing", what we learn in formal education, at school, at work, in the practical and theoretical experiences of life. It refers to that knowledge that is engraved in one's mind, based on one's experience (accumulated experience) and study. It comes from knowing, improving, clarifying individually what you didn't know. We can possess or acquire this knowledge in different ways, by studying, reading, talking, through the internet or just through our experiences. Knowledge is the basis, but just having the knowledge and not acting on it or being able to manipulate it is not enough; a professional attitude is required (ZARIFIAN, 2001).

In this way, an individual must develop a set of skills in order to achieve a certain competence. These skills must be developed during a teaching-learning process that is aimed not only at memorizing facts and dates, but also at reasoning, understanding and considering the context and situation. Skills are associated with "knowing how to do", a physical or mental action that indicates an acquired ability. Thus, identifying variables, understanding phenomena, relating information, analyzing situations, synthesizing, judging and manipulating are examples of skills. They are the technical abilities to carry out a given task, developed through theory and practice.

Attitudes, in turn, are associated with "knowing how to act", which is the individual's ability to use their skills and knowledge to generate practical results, to solve problems that arise, and to adapt their knowledge to a situational context.

Such a definition of competence is important in order to understand what knowledge, skills and attitudes are not only expected of the designer by the various members of a multidisciplinary network, and by the designer himself about his professional activity, but also what is actually performed in the practice of his activity.

Still on the subject of competencies, it is important for this work that their definition is not restricted to technical competencies alone, since these are not the only competencies mobilized for a designer to work in a group. In these social arrangements, such as a team, it is important to understand the concept of social competence, which although it is a clear concept in common sense (for example, when someone is said to have a "knack for dealing with people"), distinct from intelligence, a scientific definition of this concept is not easy.

According to Asendorpf (2004), the concept of social competence includes two distinct groups of abilities, making it a heterogeneous concept: on the one hand, the ability to impose oneself in social situations, i.e. the ability to defend one's own interests, and on the other hand, the ability to build relationships, i.e. the ability to initiate positive relationships and maintain them (ASENDORPF, 2004) by managing conflicts and enhancing skills.

Socially competent action therefore requires a person to be able to defend their interests without forgetting that they are in a relationship with other people. Thorndike (1920) calls these two aspects of social competence social sensitivity - the ability to put oneself in someone else's shoes - and social action skills - the ability to deal with difficult social situations (THORNDIKE,1920).

Competence can therefore be understood as reasoned and assertive action in the face of new challenges. This action should add economic value for the organization and social value for the individual. Competence is therefore the potential available to meet the challenges of the present and the future (ZARIFIAN, 2001).

Designers tend to experiment earlier with alternative solutions that help them better understand the problem-solution space (SCHON, 1983). In this experimentation they tend to change objectives and constraints during the design process in order to avoid significantly altering the fundamental concept and thus having to start all over again. This conversation that takes place from initial drawings and sketches has been defined by Schon (1983) as reflection in action, where he can appreciate and evaluate a solution to a problem while the process develops. However, considering the complexity of design work and as Simon (1982) has already stated about bounded rationality, not everything can be tested and measured, so the designer needs to rely on their intuition and make a choice.

Having understood the concept of competence and reflection on action, it is necessary to address in this theoretical review on competences the concepts presented by Nigel Cross, one of the scholars who has done the most in-depth studies on designer skills.

Nigel Cross (1992) defines design ability as "a multifaceted cognitive skill possessed to some degree by everyone". There are particular ways of knowing, thinking and acting that are specific to the designer (CROSS, 1992). This author draws attention to the fact that designers reason and think through drawing and sketches, which are used as a means of exploring the problem-solution space. The designer draws a line and the line talks back to the designer giving him suggestions on how to proceed (CROSS, 1992). It is important to understand this principle as a fundamental concept for making the project coherent. This way of acting provides a starting point for exploring the design problem-solution space.

CROSS (1992, 1995) developed a critique based on summarizing research into the nature of designer capabilities. In this analysis, designer capability is defined as what a designer needs to be able to accomplish. In short, Cross argues that designers should be able to:

- Produce unexpected stories and solutions;

- Tolerate uncertainty and working with incomplete or ill-defined information;

- Apply imagination and constructive forethought to practical problems;

- Use drawings and other media as a means of modeling problem solving;

- Solving ill-defined problems;

- Adopt strategies focusing on solutions;

- Use abductive thinking

- Use of non-verbal resources, graphics / media / spatial modeling.

- Work with several alternative design solutions in parallel in order to understand the problem-solution space (CROSS, 1992).

Another study that sought to identify the skills of the designer was developed by Lowgren and Stolterman (1998) who sought to separate the craft of design with its skills and body of knowledge from the ability that a designer needs to be efficient. Admitting design as the process that, according to resource constraints, is organized in order to shape and decide all the properties (functional, structural, ethical and aesthetic) of an object for a client, they conclude that the designer needs a number of different skills which are:

- Shaping something requires creative and analytical skills;

- Deciding requires critical thinking;

- Working with clients requires rationality and communication skills;

- Designing functional properties requires insight and knowledge of use.

- Designing structural properties requires discernment and knowledge of the technology;

- Ethical property design requires a vision and knowledge of values and ideals.

- Designing aesthetic properties requires the ability to shape and compose. (LOWGREN AND STOLTERMAN,1998)

It can be seen in the studies cited that both Cross (1995, 1998) and Lowgren and Stolterman (1998) seek to identify a type of design intelligence, a peculiar way for designers to think and act, an intelligence based on skills or what will be referred to in this research as competencies.

As Cross (1992) states, when sketching, the designer must deal with different levels of abstraction, which simultaneously allow him to think about the fundamental concept of the project, while reflecting on critical details.

Drawing is the activity that allows the designer to move freely between different levels of detail, which is important, especially in the early stages of the process. Designers also use sketches to identify problems and as cues to remember important information that is perceived about the problem and that can help in some way in constructing a solution. Another fundamental characteristic of sketching cited by Cross (1992) is that it aids problem structuring through trial-and-error solving and, finally, that it promotes the recognition of emergent features and properties of the solution concept that is to be developed.

Designers have an often underestimated contribution to make to the teams in which they work. Most of the time, the designer's skills allow teams to span complex boundaries, such as between departments, for example marketing and R&D; between specialties, for example hardware and software engineering, and even across organizational boundaries, when several organizations have collaborated. However, designers are still not seen as key members of these teams, and are often not even aware of their contribution and potential. On the contrary, it is the practice of design that allows this limit to be understood and expanded (STOMPFF, 2012).

With their intrinsic skills of imagination, user-centered focus and expression, which allow them to choose different languages and techniques of expression that facilitate understanding, the designer can act as an interpreter between the world of business and the world of production and technology. In this way, the designer can sketch and prototype what he or she interprets, what the intended product is based on the choices and characteristics of its users (STOMPFF, 2012). Therefore, another of the designer's skills is needed, the ability to interpret complex contexts.

2.5 ON ORGANIZATIONAL CULTURE

On the subject of organizational culture and its influence on the role of the designer, it is important to understand the recent changes in society and consequently in the environment of organizations. The contemporary world is witnessing a period of major social, political and economic transformations on a global scale. These radical transformations affect every country in the world with the irreversible phenomenon of globalization. This reality also affects design activity in the organizational environments in which it operates. Therefore, understanding the context of organizations is appropriate for this research, since this study aims to understand the activity of design and its practitioner, the designer, within an organization, specifically working in teams with professionals from other areas of knowledge.

In this sense, it is important to realize that organizational flexibility, which corresponds to the organization's ability to react to the upheavals imposed by innovation movements, represents one of the competitive advantages in market competition. Adaptations to organizational structures have a significant impact on the way in which work is organized (MARX, 1997), where one of the alternatives to this impact is the formation of work teams, teams understood here simply as social groups with integrated professional activities.

For Schein (1984), creator of the concept of organizational culture, culture is

> "a pattern of basic Shared issues that a group has learned as a way of solving its problems of external adaptation and internal integration, and which works well enough to be considered valid and desirable to be passed on to new members as the correct way of perceiving, thinking and feeling in relation to those problems" (SCHEIN, 1984).

In this way, organizational culture can also be defined as the customary or traditional way of thinking and doing things, shared to a large extent by all members of the organization and which new members must learn and accept in order to be accepted into the service of the firm". In other words, organizational culture represents the informal and unwritten norms that guide the behaviour of the members of an organization on a day-to-day basis and that direct their actions towards achieving the organizational objectives.

It is the culture that defines the mission and causes the birth and establishment of the organization's objectives. Culture needs to be aligned with other aspects of the organization's decisions and actions, such as planning, organization, direction and control, in order to better understand the organization.

In fact, culture is the way in which each organization has learned to deal with its environment. It is a complex mixture of assumptions, beliefs, behaviours, stories, myths, metaphors and other ideas that together represent the particular way an organization functions and works.

As defined by Schein (1984):

> Every culture exists on three different levels of presentation: artifacts, shared values and basic assumptions.
>
> Artifacts. They constitute the first level of culture, the most superficial, visible and perceptible. They are the things that everyone sees, hears and feels when they encounter an organization whose culture is unfamiliar. Artifacts are all those things that together define a culture and reveal how the culture pays attention to them. They include products, services and the behaviour patterns of the members of an organization.
>
> Shared values. These are the second level of culture. They are the relevant values that become important to people and define the reasons why they do what they do. They function as justifications accepted by all members. In many organizational cultures, values are originally created by the founders of the organization.
>
> Basic assumptions. These constitute the third level of organizational culture, the most intimate, profound and hidden. They are the unconscious beliefs, perceptions, feelings and dominant assumptions in which the members of the organization believe. Culture prescribes "the right way of doing things" adopted in the organization, often through unwritten and unspoken assumptions (SCHEIN, 1984).

Artifacts, shared values among members and basic assumptions constitute the main elements for knowing and understanding an organization's culture.

The formation of organizational culture brings together elements such as management parameters, philosophy and values, as well as human capital. Each individual has a different way of thinking, principles and beliefs. Bringing these people together within the same organization leads to a condensation of all these different thoughts, forming a single culture for everyone to be guided by. The dominant culture takes a macro view of the organization and deals only with core values. In the formation of the culture there is also a strong influence from the founders of the institution, who established cultural guidelines, and who are viewed with respect or even adored by a large part of the employees.

In addition to this main culture, there are also subcultures, which may or may not be related to each other, or which may even compete with each other. They can be geographical, departmental or situational. The core values of the dominant culture are present in these subcultures, but additional and particular values of certain groups, teams or departments are included.

2.6 ON TEAMS AND MULTIDISCIPLINARITY

In the context of modern organizations, the terms team and multidisciplinarity need to be discussed because they relate directly to the practical work of the designer in contemporary times.

A team can be defined as a group of people with a high degree of interdependence who are directed towards achieving a goal or completing a task (PARKER, 1995). In other words, team members agree on a goal and agree that the only way to achieve that goal is to work together.

Another scholar on teams from the field of psychology, Moscovici, states that the multiplication of human talent adds to the team and says that a group becomes a team when it starts to pay attention to its own way of operating and tries to solve the problems that affect its functioning (Moscovici, 1999). According to the same author, when diverse knowledge is brought together in order to develop a complex solution, it can be understood that a multidisciplinary team is formed.

As Morin (1999) states:

> multidisciplinarity aims to analyze each element individually and each professional seeks to express the specific opinion of his or her specialty in order to compose an integrated solution that addresses a given problem (MORIN, 1999).

For example, a digital system requires a team of system analysts, programmers, copywriters and graphic designers to build.

According to Brown (2010), these spaces (multidisciplinary teams) are where the practice of design takes place and where the designer has the opportunity to act as a mediator in a complex scenario. In this way, design, once understood as a technical activity in the area of design, and now as a multidisciplinary activity with a systemic vision, is being challenged to solve much more complex issues and is taking on a strategic position in companies. These, in turn, are increasingly recruiting designers to create ideas at the start of the development process rather than to make an already developed idea more attractive (Brown, 2009).

To solve increasingly complex issues, therefore, Brown (2009) observes that the solitary designer is being replaced by multidisciplinary teams, so that everyone develops their potential in favor of a common goal. With regard to the differences between multidisciplinary and interdisciplinary teams, it is interesting to note the difference pointed out by Brown:

> In a multidisciplinary team, each person defends his or her own technical specialty and the project becomes a protracted negotiation between team members, probably resulting in concessions against their will. In an interdisciplinary team, everyone owns the ideas and takes responsibility for them (Brown, 2009).

Brown (2009) considers that, over time, designers have developed the skills to integrate human needs and available technical resources to solve our current problems, but that, as they become concerned with meeting fundamental human needs, they can help to chart a path to a better future. Still according to Brown (2009), design thinking can and should be developed and disseminated among people who have never before thought of acting as designers, and points out that its rise is due to a cultural change where the most exciting challenge is to apply these skills to really relevant issues and thereby improve people's lives.

This interdisciplinary and integrative nature of design makes it the intersection between various areas of knowledge. According to Manzini (2008), in a world where design is an increasingly diffuse activity, being a designer in the professional sense of the term means interacting with other non-professional designers in a partnership model, using the specific knowledge of design and its tools to facilitate convergence towards shared ideas and potential solutions (i.e. proposing solutions and/or scenarios; making effective formulations based on what emerges from group discussions; developing the ideas that have been converged between partners).

However, for the team to function as such, an essential attitude is needed: collaboration. The clear and practical intention to collaborate with other professionals from different areas of knowledge in order to increase the effectiveness of the solution being developed. In this sense, I present concepts from authors in the field of management Camarinha,

Matos and Afsarmanesh (2007) and Camarinha, Matos et al. (2009) to support this theme, which is relevant to this research.

These authors classify collaboration in organizations as a process that can take place in three different ways: networking, coordination and cooperation. According to these authors, collaboration can be classified in the following ways:

> (1) Networking - involves communicating and exchanging information for mutual benefit. A simple example of networking is where a group of entities share information about their experience of using a specific tool. They may benefit from the information made available and shared, but there is not necessarily a common goal or structure that influences the form and timing of individual contributions and therefore no common value is generated;
>
> (2) Coordination - Coordination is working in harmony, which is one of the main components of collaboration. However, each entity can have a different objective and can use its own resources and methods to create value;
>
> (3) Cooperation - Not only involves exchanging information and adjusting activities, but also sharing resources to achieve compatible goals. Cooperation is achieved by sharing the work of a few (non-extensive) participants;
>
> (4) Collaboration - A process in which entities share information, resources and responsibilities, jointly planning, implementing and evaluating a program of activities to achieve a common goal. This process can be seen as a process of shared creation, therefore a process through which a group of entities strengthen their capabilities together. This implies the sharing of risks, resources, responsibilities and rewards desired by the group, giving an outside observer the image of a common identity.
>
> (CAMARINHA et al., 2009)

Collaboration can therefore be defined as a joint effort between one or more members of any structural variation or composition, based on an agreement on a common objective, surrounded by rules and governance for the construction of indicators and the monitoring of their management, which is indicated as a collaborative entity or collaborative effort.

In the development of complex solutions, typical of the contemporary society we live in today, such as an information technology solution, collaborating then refers to sharing the creation process with one or more individuals with complementary skills interacting to establish a shared understanding of the problem and a joint construction of the solution.

The concept of collaboration adopted in this research sees users and others involved in the project as active participants in the design process. This involvement takes place from the earliest stages of design projects to their most enduring stages. The design team is therefore made up of agents with design expertise and agents without such training. This approach states that each of these stakeholders has their own perspective on the arrangements of the context in question and including them in the project is a way of bringing relevant information that cannot be reached by others who are distant from the reality in which they operate.

Having finished the chapter on the theoretical framework of this research, we will now present the method chosen to carry it out.

## 2.7 HUMAN-CENTERED DESIGN (HDD), USER-CENTERED DESIGN (UCD)

## AND INTERACTION DESIGN

As this is an information technology company that develops interactive information systems such as websites, portals and web service systems, it is important to reflect on two approaches that can help us understand the design activity in these contexts, which are human-centered design, *user-centered* design and interaction design.

As presented by Krippendorff (2000):

> The focus on the human being came about at the beginning of the 1950s when the hitherto mass-produced products with functionalist characteristics, belonging to the industrial era, came to be considered consumer goods, information and identity. Designers realized that products were not things, but had become social practices, preferences and symbols, and that they would no longer meet the needs of rational users, but of buyers, consumers and certain audiences. Thus, HCD is concerned with the way people see, interpret and live with artifacts (KRIPPENDORFF, 2000).

In this way, it considers aspects relating to human characteristics and places these aspects at the heart of the design process.

Complementing this view, another design scholar presents a definition of human-centered design (HCD). For Brown (2008) it is

> a methodology that imbues the entire spectrum of innovation-related activities with the fundamental values of human-centered design (BROWN, 2008).

According to Brown (2008), the HCD approach shows that innovation, along with business and technology, must also be a factor related to human needs, behavior and preferences. Through observation, HCD captures unexpected *insights* and produces innovations that reflect exactly what consumers want.

In his book, User-Centered System Design, Norman (2006) uses the term user-centered design to describe design based on the needs of the user of a solution (product/service), leaving aside what he deems secondary, issues such as aesthetics. According to Norman (2006):

> *User-centered* design involves simplifying the structure of tasks, making things visible, matching controls and functionalities, exploiting the power of limitations and designing for error (NORMAN, 2006).

According to Norman (2006):

> user-centered design starts from a philosophy based on the needs and interests of the user, paying special attention to the issue of making products understandable and easily usable (NORMAN, 2006).

Slightly different from human-centered design, user-centered design creates an excellent user experience for products/services because it focuses on who the end user of the solution is, how and where they use it, and what their goals are. To answer these questions, UCD (*user-centered* design) uses knowledge of the skills, desires and needs of the end user to create the architecture, features and even the aesthetics of a product, such as a software interface.

As a structured approach to software development, UCD has many variations, but they are all based on a better understanding of the relationship between the product/service and its users. The ultimate goal is to adapt the product/service to the end user and their environment, not the other way around.

These concepts are directly related to the activity of the designers who will be investigated in this research, which justifies their presentation in this theoretical framework.

Two definitions can help to understand what is defined as interaction design. It can be understood as the design of interactive products that provide support for people's daily activities, whether at home or at work (SHARP, ROGERS and PREECE, 2002). Complementing this vision, it can also be understood as the design of spaces for human communication and interaction (WINOGRAD, 1997).

Interaction Design is the area of design whose main focus is the design of interfaces and interactive devices, such as desktop and mobile applications and digital games. This recent field of design deals not only with human-machine interfaces (Human-Computer Interface), but also with the use of computers as a means of communication between individuals. It is up to the interaction designer to analyze and understand the actions of the end user of the solution they are designing, knowing the extent of their senses, their needs and expectations in relation to the object or environment.

Interaction projects must guide experiences, taking into account the ethnography of the user and their social, cultural and economic aspects. Their activity lies in an area of intersection between new technologies and human actions. At this intersection is the designer who designs the interfaces of these devices, which will be observed in this research.

The scientific research method and techniques chosen for this research will be presented below.

# 3. METHODOLOGY

To carry out this research, a case study with a qualitative and exploratory approach, and also because there were two different audiences to be investigated, designers and non-designers, two information-gathering techniques were used, one for each audience. For designers, the technique chosen was the focus group and for non-designers, the technique chosen was in-depth interviews.

It's important to point out that before choosing this information-gathering technique, the most appropriate term would be to consider that, in addition to simply gathering information, what will take place in this research is akin to building information. Here we will consider the information generated by the research - as already partially constructed from the first moment of its identification. Therefore, it is not really a question of collection, as if the data were there, passive, waiting to be captured, but rather of capturing the meanings that emerge during the research situation and the implementation of the research techniques, as the participants reflect on and discuss the proposed theme.

Initially, the idea was to use participant observation for this study because it was thought that this would be the most appropriate methodological option for carrying out an exploratory qualitative study of this nature, and perhaps it was. However, this choice proved to be complex to apply and unfeasible due to the time available to carry out the research.

Another complicating factor was the fact that the researcher was an employee of the organization being studied, which would make it difficult to achieve the strangeness and distance from the field that is necessary for participant observation to be carried out fully and efficiently, and also because of the difficulty in finding the time to carry out this type of observation.

## 3.1 DESIGNERS

For the investigation into designers, we sought to use an information-gathering technique that would take advantage of the researcher's familiarity with the field under study and with the individuals who would take part in the technique, so that this familiarity would generate greater spontaneity on the part of the participants and enhance the veracity of the information provided during the research techniques. Another factor that influenced the choice of the focus group technique was the possibility of bringing together a group of individuals from the same profession, with the same profile, which seemed more appropriate.

We also looked for a technique that could be applied more quickly than participant observation and that would produce similar results. In this sense, the focus group technique was chosen to be applied to designers, as it was believed that a group conversation on a central theme (focus), the opinions and collective constructions of meaning of a class of professionals could be more evident and closer to reality, especially when it is about oneself, in this case designers reflecting on the condition of being a designer, role and competencies.

What characterizes the focus group technique is the explicit use of group interaction to produce data and insights that would be less accessible without group interaction. The main advantage of the focus group is the opportunity to observe a large amount of interaction on a topic in a limited period of time.

The focus group does not seek consensus, but rather a plurality of ideas. Thus, the emphasis is on interaction within the group, based on topics offered by the researcher, who takes on the role of moderator. The main interest is to recreate a social context or environment where the individual can interact with others, defending, revising, ratifying their own opinions or influencing the opinions of others. This approach also allows the researcher to deepen their understanding of the answers obtained.

### 3.1.1 Procedure

Below is a description of the procedure adopted for applying the focus group technique in the organization studied, detailing aspects relating to the researcher moderator, the selection of participants and the script of questions that guided the discussion. The focus group technique was applied with the designers of the company studied in August 2014.

3.1.1.1 Participant selection

The individuals participating in the focus group were chosen according to the theme and objectives of the research. Although Morgan (1997) recommends using people who are strangers to each other to make up the group, the experience reported in this article contradicts this recommendation, as we will see later, not least because the study takes place within a sector of an organization where people naturally know each other. Moreover, applied research carried out within organizations makes the participation of people who know each other inevitable and often even desirable.

According to Vichas (apud GIOVINAZZO, 2001):

> the groups must be homogeneous in terms of certain parameters defined according to the topic and objectives of the research to be carried out. This homogeneity favors

identification and integration between participants, avoiding radically conflicting positions between group members. However, it is often the contrasting perspectives and points of view of the participants that are of interest, so a certain amount of heterogeneity is required in the composition of the focus group. It is clear that, paradoxically, the sample needs to be homogeneous and heterogeneous at the same time and, in order to achieve these qualities, it is necessary to define criteria that facilitate this differentiation (Vichas apud GIOVINAZZO, 2001).

In the case of this research, homogeneity was achieved in the sense that all the designers invited to take part in the focus group were designers. However, a certain amount of heterogeneity was also achieved due to the fact that the designers invited had different levels of experience and ages, some being recent graduates, others trainees, others with more than 10 years' experience and others with more than 20 years' experience. This difference provided different points of view on the same central question that guided the research, generating an in-depth reflection on the role and competencies of the designer in multidisciplinary teams from the point of view of the context studied.

It is also important to note that this experiment was authorized by a document signed by the head of the sector and the division manager, which represented the company's official consent to carry out the research and the experiment (appendix A). In addition to this official authorization from the organization, each informant selected to take part in the focus group received a consent form (appendix C) to be read and signed before taking part in the focus group experiment, setting out the terms for using the content discussed, as well as the researcher's commitment to keeping the informants' identities confidential.

Normally, each company establishes its own name and classification for each position. Most companies classify a professional's career as: trainee, junior, full, senior, master and specialist. This classification is usually based on the length of experience within a company. In the organization studied, the classification by level of experience is as follows:

3.1.1.2 Classification used at PROCERGS

Table 1 - Classification of the level of experience in the job applied at PROCERGS

| Level | Length of experience | Training | Responsibilities |
|---|---|---|---|
| Trainee | Less than 1 year | Studying for a degree | Tasks of small or medium complexity in specific area(s) with supervision. |
| Junior (JR) | Up to 5 years | Recent graduate | Simple procedural functions or those that do not require in-depth knowledge of an area of activity |

| | | | |
|---|---|---|---|
| Pieno (PL) | 6 to 9 years | Postgraduate | Specific activities requiring in-depth knowledge. Makes decisions endorsed by a superior. |
| Senior (SR) | From 10 years old | Postgraduate Manager | +Makes decisions. Acts autonomously, based on the knowledge and experience acquired throughout their career. Manages people and projects. |
| Master | 15 years or older | Postgraduate + Manager Certifications | Works outside the supervisory process or on +demand. Manages projects/business. Has full autonomy. |

### 3.1.1.3  Profile of the participants

To carry out this research, seven designers were selected who were employees of the company: 2 of senior level (more than 10 years working as a designer) who were named informant 1 and informant 7); 1 of full level (with between 6 and 9 years working as a designer) named informant 4; 1 junior designer (with less than 5 years working) named Informant 3; 3 design trainees, one of whom was just finishing his degree course, called informant 2, and the other two were halfway through their degree course in design, called informants 5 and 6 respectively.

These professionals were contacted individually by e-mail and also in person about their request to take part in the study, when they were informed of the objectives of the study and who would conduct the technique and how it would be carried out. They were also informed by these means about the official authorizations provided by the company through the head and management to carry out the research and release the employees to take part in the scientific experiment.

### 3.1.1.4  Focus group application script

The focus group presupposes, as its name suggests, the existence of a focus, or central theme for discussion, around which people will air their ideas, perceptions and feelings. In this research, this focus was the role of the designer working in multidisciplinary teams and the skills needed to perform this role. For this to happen effectively, the discussion process had to be carefully planned, sequencing the aspects of the topic to be discussed.

The topics were organized and scripted according to the logical scheme deemed most appropriate for the research in question.

This script revolved around the central theme of the research, raising questions related to the role of the designer and the skills needed to fulfill this role. These questions served to guide the group discussion, so that all the participants could naturally and spontaneously provide relevant information related to the research objectives, resulting in a collective construction of information, meanings and knowledge on the subject.

This measure helped the moderator/researcher to orient himself during the session, giving him greater control over the situation. The script, although important as a guide to the discussion, cannot be inflexible as a "straitjacket" that forces the group to discuss more extensively a topic that clearly doesn't interest them or to move on to another topic when they still have something to say about the issue being examined.

This survey was based on a script with 6 basic questions, which were clarified by sub-items when necessary. These questions were discussed with the group for 1 hour and 50 minutes.

A first group was used as a pilot group, with students from the master's degree in design at UNISINOS (three students plus the research supervisor), where the questionnaire could be perfected in terms of its shortcomings before being applied to the study group for this research. The test was of fundamental importance so that the questions could be clarified, and it was possible to identify questions that were still unclear in the script or that could generate some kind of misunderstanding, holding up the process of the focus group conversation or diverting the focus of the conversation. In this way, it was possible to adjust the questions, making the discussion more fluid and going straight to the central issue, the focus of the research, as required by a focus group, enabling the researcher to check that the questions were appropriate to the time allotted for each answer and the instructions given to the participants.

The script to be applied in this survey will address the following main questions: 1 - How did you become interested in the profession of designer? 2 - What do you think a person needs to possess or know in order to work as a designer? 3 - Do you think a designer works better alone or in a team? Why? 4 - What do you see as the main purpose and objective of a designer as a professional? 5 - If you were to describe a designer to someone who had never heard of them, how would you describe them? Explain and 6 - Do you think that the organizational culture of the company influences the role of the designer? in what way? The complete script is attached to this dissertation (Appendix B).

3.1.1.5 Focus group application protocol

To conduct the sessions, the researcher opted for the following organization: One (1) moderator/researcher responsible for the recording equipment and for controlling the time; Seven (7) designers who are employees of the company and work as designers, who were selected and informed in advance about the experiment.

When the moderator began working with the group, he adopted the following protocol:

•	He introduced himself and thanked everyone for their participation;

•	He explained the aim of the meeting, the research topic and the general and specific objectives of the study;

•	She was informed about the consent form for taking part in the research;

•	He informed us about the audio and video recording of the focus group, explaining that there would be confidentiality of the information, the use of the data and the anonymity of the participants, as only members of the research team would have access to the transcriptions.

•	I asked to be seen as a researcher, an external agent and not as a colleague, during the focus group, so that the participants could express themselves without any fear of a company colleague.

•	He informed us about the dynamics of the focus group, the questions that would guide the discussion and the time available to carry out the practice.

•	At the end of the practice session, the moderator thanked everyone for taking part, left room for further discussion and announced that a new meeting would be scheduled after the end of the research to present and discuss the results obtained, so that the knowledge generated in the research could be applied to improving and expanding the role and work of the designer within the organization.

3.1.1.6  Recording information from the focus group

The focus group discussion was recorded on audio using two voice recorders (cell phone apps) and was also recorded on video using a portable high-definition camera (Go Pro) that was fixed in a discreet place in the meeting room where the discussion took place, on *full HD* video with audio, both operated by the mediator/researcher.

It is important to mention that the use of audio and video together helped a great deal in facilitating the subsequent transcription of the content, because during the transcription of the content, at times when the audio was not so clear, it was possible to clarify what was being said by analyzing the image recorded on video. In this way, the use of two tools to record the technique provided a more complete observation of the interaction that took place, generating a greater understanding of the information that was generated in the focus group discussion.

To hold the focus group, a company meeting room was booked for two hours with a central meeting table and comfortable chairs where everyone could sit back and relax. All the participants were booked as normal for any work meeting in the organization, with the prior authorization of their bosses and managers. So everything took place like a normal day-to-day company meeting. This seemed to have worked satisfactorily, as the discussion went on in a relaxed manner, covering all the topics and when it was over the participants didn't notice the time passing and were still willing to talk more about the subject.

3.1.1.7 Information saturation of the focus group

According to Mattar (apud GIOVINAZZO, 2001), the ideal size for groups should be between 8 and 12 people. In the case of this research, a focus group of seven people plus the moderator/researcher was used, totaling eight people in the focus group within the number indicated by Mattar (apud GIOVINAZZO, 2001). This number proved to be significant, as it was intended to bring together most of the designers from the organization studied in a broad discussion on the research topic.

Finally, it's important to note that the choice of participants for the focus group brought together more than 88% of the designers in the company, which currently has 9 designers in a universe of 1200 employees from the most diverse areas working in multidisciplinary teams made up of analysts, programmers, business analysts, marketing analysts, administration, information technology and managers.

3.2 NO DESIGNERS

As the central theme of this research is the role and competencies of the designer working in multidisciplinary teams, it was felt that it would be important to gather not only the perceptions of the designers themselves about their profession, role and competencies, but also the perceptions of non-designers who work in these same teams together with designers, as it is believed that these views are complementary on the subject.

However, in order to capture non-designers' views on the role and skills of designers, the focus group technique proved to be unfeasible due to the difficulty of bringing non-designers together to discuss the subject and also because different views on working with designers were perceived beforehand. These differences indicated the need for a more flexible, objective research technique that sought to gather direct information from the source under investigation. A technique that would also allow the individual being investigated to construct their own view of the subject more deeply and personally, without the influence or interference of others, as occurs in group research techniques.

Therefore, with the non-designers, the data collection/construction technique chosen was semi-structured in-depth interviews, a qualitative technique that explores a subject by seeking information, perceptions and direct experiences reported by selected informants and guided by a pre-established script of questions on the subject in order to analyze and present them in a structured way.

Considering that in organizational studies, as is the case with this research, it is necessary to integrate thematization and depth in order to understand the complexity of the phenomena and the relationships that permeate them, we opted for semi-structured in-depth interviews as the method of data collection to be applied to non-designers. The exploratory nature of this type of interview makes them suitable for any type of investigation, but they are especially useful when investigating sensitive subjects and subjects where there is little knowledge about them and which you want to explore, as in this case study.

In the case of this research, the interviewer was the researcher himself. Together with his supervisor, the researcher determined a set of questions that formed the interview script. As well as having a structured script, the researcher took some preparatory steps that proved to be very important in making the semi-structured in-depth interview technique possible.

Those selected to take part were contacted by e-mail and in person. A request for official authorization from the head of the sector and the division's management (appendix 3) to carry out the experiment and release the employee to participate, distribution of the consent form for the use of the content recorded during the experiment for later content analysis and presentation as research results, as well as a guarantee of confidentiality regarding the identities of the informants.

Below is a description of the interview procedure used in this research.

### 3.2.1 Procedure

The following is a description of the procedure adopted for applying the semi-structured in-depth interviews in the organization studied, detailing aspects relating to the selection of participants, the script of questions that guided the discussion, the protocol for applying the interviews, recording the content and saturation of the sample.

3.2.1.1 Participant selection

To conduct the interviews, seven non-designers were selected from the company studied, who interact in the project teams with the designers, occupying different positions such as sector head and manager (management), systems analysts, programmers and business analysts (commercial sector), distributed as follows: 2 master systems analysts and managers (division and sector) named respectively informants 1 and 2; 2 full systems analysts named informant 4 and 5; 2 business analysts, one full and one master named respectively informant 3 and 7; junior programmer named informant 6.

Once again, homogeneity was sought in the sense that they were all individuals who interact professionally with the designer in the development of projects and company demands, and who therefore have significant information about the role, skills and image of the design professional.

Heterogeneity, on the other hand, was achieved by selecting professionals from different areas (business, systems analysis, management and programming) and also from different levels within the company, ranging from a novice programmer to a division manager analyst.

The interviews used in this research were considered in-depth and semi-structured, as they were based on a script of questions that guided the interview.

3.2.1.2 Semi-structured in-depth interview questionnaire

The semi-structured in-depth interview applied in this research was based on a matrix, a script of guiding questions that aimed to cover the research interest. This list of questions originated from the research problem, the role and competencies of the designer working in multidisciplinary teams, and sought to address the breadth of the topic, presenting each question as openly as possible.

This script of broad, open questions was constructed based on the theme and objectives of the research and tested beforehand with two pilot interviewees. The test made it possible to improve the questions in the script in order to make it easier to understand the questions and for the interviewees to express themselves freely. After the tests and adjustments to the questionnaire, the interviews were carried out individually with each of the selected non-designers, so that each of them could give their in-depth version of the issues relating to the research problem in question.

The researcher therefore drew up a questionnaire containing the following main questions: 1 - What do you think is the importance of a designer? 2 - What do you think a person needs to have in order to work as a designer? and to work as a designer at PROCERGS?

3 - Do you think a designer works better alone or in a team? Why? 4 - If you were to describe a designer to someone who had never heard of them, how would you describe them? and 5 - Do you think that the company's organizational culture influences the role of the designer? in what way? The full interview script is attached to this dissertation (appendix 2).

### 3.2.1.3 Interview protocol

Each interview was previously arranged and scheduled individually with each participant. They were first contacted in person and invited to take part and then, after accepting the personal invitation, they were contacted by e-mail, when they were informed of the location (meeting room), the day and time of the interview, the objectives of the work and the official authorizations of the company and managers to carry out the experiment.

The interviews took place between August and October 2014. 7 interviews were scheduled with the selected individuals who readily agreed to take part in the research. These interviews were scheduled in the meeting rooms of the company studied. Each appointment reserved a room for an hour, so that the interview, which was scheduled to take an average of 40 minutes, could take place in a calm and unhurried manner.

The average length of the interviews was 30 minutes. However, some interviews were shorter and more direct, lasting 25 minutes, and others were more extensive and discussed, lasting up to 45 minutes.

### 3.2.1.4 Recording information

The interviews were recorded only in audio, using voice recorders in cell phone applications (in this case, two cell phones were used per guarantee), unlike the focus group, which also used video as a recording resource.

In the case of the interviews, it was decided to use only audio recordings and to do so discreetly, in order to make the interviewee feel more comfortable in giving their answers and opinions on the subject. It was also deemed unnecessary to use video because the proximity of the researcher and the interviewee in an interview is greater, making it less necessary to use a complementary means of recording to better understand the answers given to the questions.

### 3.2.1.5 Information saturation of semi-structured in-depth interviews

The size of the sample of non-designers to be interviewed was defined on the basis of certain criteria, in order to seek a balance between the sample of designers and non-designers to be investigated. In this way, the same number of non-designers were selected, seven, thus achieving a quantitative balance of individuals.

## 3.3 CONTENT ANALYSIS - TECHNIQUE FOR PROCESSING COLLECTED AND CONSTRUCTED INFORMATION

After the focus group meetings and interviews were over, the researcher transcribed the audio recordings and analyzed the information produced using a qualitative approach using the **content analysis** technique, where analysis categories were defined for the transcribed content**, which was** selected according to its importance in relation to the research objectives.

According to Moraes (1990):

> Content analysis is a research method used to describe and interpret the content of all kinds of documents and texts. It leads to systematic descriptions, whether qualitative or quantitative, and helps to reinterpret messages and reach an understanding of their meanings at a level that goes beyond a common reading. By using this interpretative part of the content, it comes closer to the concept already explained at the beginning of the method chapter of this research of the joint construction of information and not just a simple collection of data (MORAES, 1990).

As a research method, content analysis comprises special procedures for processing scientific data. It is a tool, a practical guide to action, which is always being renewed in the light of the increasingly diverse problems it sets out to investigate. It can be thought of as a single instrument, but marked by a great variety of forms and adaptable to a very wide field of application, such as design for example (MORAES, 1990).

In the case of this research, the information was transcribed from the audio and video recordings of the focus group with the designers and only the audio recordings made during the interviews with the non-designers. All these recordings were transcribed into text so that they could undergo content analysis. The focus group with the designers totaled 32 pages of transcribed text. The seven interviews conducted with non-designers totaled 54 pages of transcribed text. The sum of the two data collection techniques resulted in 86 pages of text, a wealth of content for the analysis that followed.

Content analysis, in its qualitative form, as was the case in this research, is based on a series of assumptions which, when examining a text, serve as a support for capturing its symbolic meaning. This meaning is not always manifest and its significance is not unique. It can be approached from different perspectives. For this reason, a text contains many meanings which can vary according to the text:

(a)   the meaning the author intends to express may coincide with the meaning perceived by the reader;

(b)   the meaning of the text may be different for each reader;

(c)   The same author can send a message, but different readers can take it in different ways;

(d)   a text can express a meaning of which the author himself is not aware.

It is also important to note that it will always be possible to investigate texts from multiple perspectives, as Krippendorf (1990) states in the following quote:

> In any written message, letters, words and sentences can be computed simultaneously; sentences can be categorized, the logical structure of expressions can be described, associations, denotations, connotations can be verified and psychiatric, sociological or political interpretations can also be formulated (KRIPPENDORF, 1990).

It should also be remembered that although consensus or intersubjective agreement on what a message means simplifies content analysis, this coincidence of meanings is not indispensable. The values and natural language of the interviewee and the researcher, as well as cultural language and its meanings, exert an influence on the data that the researcher cannot escape.

In a way, content analysis is a personal interpretation on the part of the researcher in relation to his perception of the data. A neutral reading is not possible. Every reading is an interpretation. This question of the multiple meanings of a message and the multiple possibilities of analysis it allows is very closely related to the context in which the communication takes place.

### 3.3.1 Content analysis procedure

Even if the documents to be examined through content analysis already exist, they need to be prepared and transformed to constitute the information to be subjected to content analysis. The data is not entirely data, but needs to be properly prepared for it. The objectives of the research play a central role in this.

So the first task after the information gathering/construction techniques had been carried out was for the researcher to transcribe the audio recordings into text format, where he had a second contact with the content, since the first contact was when the practice was carried out. This second contact already represented a re-processing of the information built up during the focus group and interview techniques.

3.3.1.1 Preparation

Once we had the transcribed information to be analyzed, we first had to subject it to a preparation process that consisted of:

(a)   Identify the different samples of information to be analyzed. To do this, all the transcribed material was read in order to make an initial decision about which units of analysis would actually be significant in relation to the research objectives and also to understand whether the categories defined a priori on the basis of Cross's (1984) study were adequate and sufficient. Therefore, this reading served as the researcher's **third contact** with the content collected, constructed and transcribed, in order to identify the most significant units of analysis according to their relationship with the theme and objectives of the research.

(b)   Start the process of coding the materials by establishing a code that would make it possible to quickly identify each element of the sample of statements or documents to be analyzed. This code was made up of numbers and letters which, from then on, guided the researcher to return to the specific document whenever he wished. In this way, the content of the focus group was duly numbered in its lines of text and according to the informant. For example (L34-I2) meaning line thirty-four of the transcript, informant two. Based on this code, it was easier to identify and access the content within the transcript, making it easier to analyze the content.

After this preparation and initial reading of the transcript contents came the second part of the analysis, which was Categorization.

3.3.1.2 Categorization

Categorization is a procedure for grouping data according to what they have in common. It classifies by similarity or analogy, according to criteria previously established or defined in the research process.

In the case of this research, the categories of analysis were defined based on the relationship between the observed units of analysis and the objectives of the research and also related to the theoretical framework of the research presented in the study by Nigel Cross (1984) where, in a similar study of observation of the designer in teams, he presented some categories of analysis that served as a basis for this research.

Still on the subject of categories, it is important to stress that they are the result of extensive selection and adaptation to the objectives of the research and the content collected, which resulted in a list of categories that was adjusted, optimized, clarified, so as to bring together only categories judged to be truly significant in relation to the objectives of the research and revolving around this main focus: the role and competencies of the designer in multidisciplinary teams.

### 3.3.1.3 Selection of analysis units

After reading the transcripts, with the categories already defined, adjusted and described, and following on from the content analysis technique, a table was constructed with the selected units of analysis placed in their respective categories. This table will be presented in the results section of this dissertation after the method chapter.

# 4. RESULTS

Before presenting the results, we should present the negotiations that took place in the organization to apply the techniques that were determined in the method, present the organization and its workflow to identify where the designer is located within the organization, the history of this professional's work within the organization, as well as present the profile of the participants in the focus group (designers) and the semi-structured in-depth interviews (non-designers).

## 4.1 PRIOR NEGOTIATIONS

Because this research was carried out in a public company with a significant presence in the market and because the informants were people who were actually carrying out their professional activities, certain measures were necessary to guarantee an ethical standard in the conduct of the study. In this way, an internal process was created, an internal company document that approved the carrying out of this study based on the approval of the managers of the sector studied, the management of the division in which this sector is located and the company's management, which realized that scientific interest in the way its professionals work could make a significant contribution to the analysis and improvement of its processes. This document is attached to this dissertation (Appendix A).

In addition to this formal authorization from the company, the head of the sector and the division to which this sector belongs were asked to make an official announcement informing the members of the teams involved in the projects being observed that a colleague would be carrying out a scientific study based on focus groups and interviews over a period of 6 to 8 months. This notice informed them of the subject of the research, how long it would last, the projects that would be observed and the professionals who would be under observation and who could be called in for interviews. The need for this official announcement with the approval of managers was due to two factors:

(1) The need to establish a differentiated relationship between the professional colleague and the observer and researcher, so that for a certain period of the day (as already mentioned in the methodology chapter) the colleague could carry out his observation with the awareness of all the members;

(2) In order to obtain greater cooperation and willingness on the part of the individuals observed to provide information on the subjects being researched, this study was officially authorized and communicated by the company's management, thus assuming an official importance and not merely a speculative and independent intention on the part of the

researcher.

After these two measures, I began discussions with the head of the sector in which I work at the company to obtain my partial release to carry out the research technique. In these conversations, I explained the subject of the research and, above all, the method and my commitment to secrecy regarding the identities of the informants.

As a result of these negotiations, as a researcher myself, I felt freer to carry out the study and, having defined the projects that would be observed, I was able to establish a timetable for both the focus group with the company's designers and the in-depth interviews with non-designers.

Therefore, before analyzing the transcribed results of the focus group and interviews, and in order to better understand the context in which the research will take place, I will give a detailed description of the field of observation (the company). In this description, based on official documents, employee testimonials and my 15 years' experience as an employee, I will try to describe the company's structure, its strategic definitions, services provided, functional and organizational structure and hierarchy, the company's workflow, the technical profile and duties of the professionals, the sector observed, the teams and projects that will be observed and the activity of design and the designer within this context. After this description, I will analyze and interpret the information collected during the observation of the projects and the interviews.

4.2 COMPANY PRESENTATION

PROCERGS - Companhia de Processamento de Dados do Estado do Rio Grande do Sul (Rio Grande do Sul State Data Processing Company), is a mixed-capital company that began operations on December 28, 1972 as the executing agency of the state's IT policy. PROCERGS is the largest IT company in Rio Grande do Sul and processes millions of transactions every day that are vital for the smooth running of the public service and for serving the community, affecting the lives of millions of people.

To meet these needs, PROCERGS has worked hand in hand with other state agencies, generating solutions that contribute to supporting government action, modernizing public management, improving the services provided to citizens and democratizing access to information, seeking to ensure that the state and the community receive the maximum return on their investments in public IT.

Below are the strategic statements in force at the company in 2014:

Business: Information and Communication Technology solutions for the Public

Administration. Mission: To provide Information and Communication Technology solutions to increase the efficiency and transparency of public services and bring government and citizens closer together. Relevant company values: Quality, Innovation, Ethics, Commitment, Trust and Solidarity. Vision and objective as an institution: To be recognized by the RS Public Administration as a benchmark and the best option in ICT solutions. (PROCERGS Strategic Planning 2013)

The company is managed by the Board of Directors and the Executive Board, which is made up of the CEO, vice-president, technical director and administrative-financial director (PROCERGS Statutes, 2011).

The company's market is limited to the State Public Administration (Direct and Indirect) of Rio Grande do Sul, agencies of the other powers of Rio Grande do Sul, as well as public or private entities, city halls, other states of the federation and the federal government with services linked to the client systems of the main market.

Entry to the company as an employee is by means of a public examination and this affects all areas of the company, but as it is a public and governmental company, management is carried out by directors appointed by the state government, in positions of trust determined by political relationships.

The company has its headquarters in the city of Porto Alegre, where this research was carried out. In addition to the headquarters building, there are six other sectors that are not located at the headquarters, which make up what are known as decentralized units. In addition to these units located in the state capital, it also has a network of regional coordinating offices in six cities in the countryside.

**4.2.1 History of designers in the company**

The inclusion of designers in the company's workforce began in the 1970s with the design department, whose main task was to format the documents used in the company. However, their importance really began to be taken into account in the 1990s with the advent of the web, which introduced the use of graphic interfaces on the web. This led the company to admit the need for people with specific knowledge of design and visual programming, who could apply their knowledge to improve the aesthetic aspect (form) and usability of web-based solutions.

The first public competition for the position of designer was held in 1994. Until then, the job was carried out by trainees and outsourced professionals or those from other areas such as technical drawing, illustration and visual programming.

The second competition for designers was held in 1997. However, in this second competition, there was still no clear definition of what knowledge a designer should have to work in the development of websites and systems, or what degree he or she should have. For this reason, in the definitions in the competition notice, the position of designer, although it was at a higher level, which would require a minimum formal study of a degree, in this competition allowed for an incomplete degree. In addition, this incomplete degree could be in the fields of architecture, social communication, industrial design and plastic arts, various fields that had some relation to creative processes, which signaled a lack of definition about the position, its origin and the role of this professional in the teams they would join.

Over the years, and with the dizzying development of the internet and all telecommunications, this role has changed. Currently, the designer's duties include the information architecture of systems and websites, visual programming, understood as the appropriate choice of the formal aspects of the solution (colors, shapes, typography, layout, usability).

In order to shed more light on the history of the designer's work in the company, I asked the company's longest-serving designer to describe his work. The result is shown in the table below:

Chart 2 - Description of the designer's role in the company as described by the longest-serving design professional

| Season | Description | Duties |
|---|---|---|
| The 70s | The Design Department was the first department to work with graphic material and photography in the company. | Document layout, |
| The 80s | Design and visual programming sector | Photography from production to developing negatives, form designs, layouts, architectural plans and various printed graphic materials. |
| The 90s | Multimedia Sector | Responsible for audio-visual presentations in IBM storybord and later in PowerPoint. Illustrations, general promotional materials and first illustrations for the Internet. |
| The 90s | Division 7 - Internet and after 1994 DPRO - Projects Division. | From 1995 Production of images and layouts for |

| | | |
|---|---|---|
| | Hiring industrial design students from UFRGS in Santa Maria to work with graphic design and the internet. | company and client websites. Production of graphic material for packaging and other materials for internal and external use. |
| The 2000s | DPRO - Design team Forming a team of designers to prospect and produce services in the field. After 2005 - Creation of the solutions development division, which attached the design sector. Subsequently, the web services sector was created, called SSW, where most of the company's designers are concentrated. | Development of websites and systems, graphic material and other design and illustration work. Web design consultancy. |
| After 2010 | Changes in the nomenclature of the divisions and sectors and in their duties: the solutions division was renamed the Software Development Division (DDS). The web services sector (SSW) now includes among its tasks the development of applications for mobile devices (tablets, notebooks, cell phones) and the adaptation of websites to these devices, applying what is known as responsive design. | Information architecture and design of websites, portals and web systems, production of images, layouts, wireframes and Responsive design of websites and systems. |

## 4.2.2 About the workflow in the company

To begin the report on the observations made during this research, I'm going to start by describing the flow of project demands in the company in order to show how the demands reach the sector.

The origin of all the demands met in the sector studied comes from four possible sources of demand: (1) the State Government, involving the Governor, the Civil House, the Communications Secretariat, State Secretariats; State agencies, companies and foundations such as FDRH, IRGA, DETRAN and the company itself through its own IT initiatives suggested by managers and business analysts.

The demands flow from requests made by secretaries, managers or advisors to the governor who contact PROCERGS when they have an IT demand. PROCERGS receives these requests through its BAs (business analysts) who contact the internal sectors to see who can take on the demand according to the priority given by the company's directors.

Once the sector that will take on the demand has been defined, a multidisciplinary team is formed consisting of AS (Systems Analyst), Designer, Programmer/Developer. After the NA has negotiated with the heads of the sectors, this project team is formed. The NA, who is responsible for the service, schedules an initial BRIEFING meeting with the client, the AS, who usually takes over project management, and the Designer.

At the *briefing* meeting, the client's needs are presented (website, system, portal, hotsite) and a new solution is created or an old one is redesigned. The *briefing* meeting is concluded and the project manager (AS) draws up a preliminary project with a survey of the hours needed by each professional to create the solution. At this stage, based on his experience and briefing, the designer presents his estimate of the hours needed to create the solution.

In this forecast, the designer presents the time needed to develop his part of the solution in hours. It's important to note that until a few years ago this initial meeting was held without the presence of the designer, but as there was a lot of disagreement about the demand and realizing that the designer's work is the first to be done in this process and with dialogue and negotiation, we increasingly realized the importance of the presence of this actor in the process. In this way, the presence of the designer at the *briefing* meeting has become a rule within the company's methodology that allows for a greater understanding of the demand/project to be developed.

The results of the researcher's field trip will be presented below, based on the two research techniques provided for in the method: focus groups with designers and semi-structured in-depth interviews with non-designers. This information will feed into the discussion that follows, along with the theoretical framework observed in this research.

4.3  CATEGORIES OF ANALYSIS - DESIGNERS (FOCUS GROUP)

In this research, the categories used a priori in Nigel Cross's study (1984) proved to be insufficient after the first reading of the transcripts of the focus group and interviews. In addition, the initial reading of the transcribed content and the objectives of this study, which are deeper and broader, in themselves demonstrated the need for other categories of analysis to cover other significant aspects mentioned during the focus group with the designers and the interviews with the non-designers.

In a previous study carried out by Nigel Cross (1984), which served as the basis for this research, designers were observed during their process and their content was recorded on audio and video and then transcribed into text, which underwent content analysis. In this study, the units of analysis were organized into categories that aided the content analysis.

In order to observe the designer-in-process working in teams to better understand their roles. The following categories emerged from Cross's study:

- **Roles and Relationships**

- **Planning and Action**

- **Capturing and sharing information**

- **Analyzing and understanding problems**

- **Concept generation and adoption**

- **Conflict management**

In order to meet the general and specific objectives of this research and based on the analysis of the content collected in the field, it was realized that these aspects were neither sufficient nor adequate for the analysis that was intended with the study that this dissertation and research deals with.

Unlike Nigel Cross's study, this research did not focus on observing designers carrying out their practical activity or fully developing their work process. The aim was to find out their opinions and expectations about their profession, their role, their competencies and the context in which they work. The aim of this study was to reflect on the role of this professional in current times, trying to identify the designer's own characteristics, expectations, concepts, pre-conceptions and post-conceptions in relation to this role and also trying to identify the competences needed and mobilized to perform this role in multidisciplinary teams and developing integrated and complex solutions.

The way to build this knowledge was to understand expectations, opinions, capture the image that design professionals themselves make of themselves when they are part of teams with professionals from other areas of knowledge, and also to capture the opinion of professionals from other areas of knowledge (classified simply as non-designers) who are part of the teams about the role and competencies of the design professional.

Therefore, although the work of Nigel Cross served as the basis for the method used in this research, more categories of analysis were necessary in order to reflect on and understand more specific details of the role and competencies of the designer working in multidisciplinary teams.

This resulted in the following groupings of categories, subcategories and units of analysis for the content analysis of this research, as shown in Table 3 below:

## 4.3.1 Table of categories, subcategories and units of analysis from the focus group with designers

Chart 3 - Categories, subcategories and units of analysis selected from the transcript of the focus group with designers

| Theme | Categories | Subcategories/Definition | Line/form | Units of Analysis |
|---|---|---|---|---|
| Papers | Duties | **Regarding the appearance/presentation of a product/service** | L 1061-1062-16<br><br>L 487 -15 | "(...) He's the guy who designs to communicate something in graphic form, some need, who cares about the appearance, the shape of the product and how it should look to delight its user."<br>"(...) So the designer's job is always to think only visually." |
| | | **Problem solving** | L 992 -15<br>L 1091-1092-12 | ""(...) Solving problems..."<br>"(...) We develop options for problems using methods specific to the area..." |
| | | **Tasks to improve user experience and people's lives.** | L 1017-1018 -13<br>L 467-468 -16<br>L 1014-1016 -13 | "(...) Getting people to do their jobs lightly and with a good experience."<br>"(...) We need to understand the person, we need to understand. And that's where the biggest challenge lies."<br>"(...) The goal... Born, globally, is to improve people's lives by doing more, with less, with less material, with less effort, that is easier, that spends less money, that is more sustainable and that, in our specific area, in communication, in the interface..." |
| | | **Attributions regarding the functionality and usability of products** | L 1026-1029-13<br>L 1252-1253-16 | "(...) Thinking of PROCERGS and the government, the best thing for us designers here would be for someone to say, "Well, I had to pay my fine there. Man, that's easy. I took my cell phone here, gave it three taps, I got it at home, show of boo", that would be the pinnacle.<br>"(...) It's just that aesthetics is there for function, you know? I don't think aesthetics is purely aesthetic, because it serves the function." |
| | | **Multidisciplinary duties** | L 1063-1064-15<br>L 366-370 -13 | "(...) A person who is connected in different aspects, different knowledge, tendencies who suddenly finds it easy to create connections between things."<br>"(...) The person's ability to do just that, to inter-relate and know all this daily knowledge, I can bring knowledge of architecture, with graphic design, with printed design, with the research I've done with people, to be able to relate and tie together all this |

| | | | | |
|---|---|---|---|---|
| | | | | that I come to do. |
| | Paper dynamics | The dynamic role of the designer | L 578- 11<br>L584-585 -12 | "(...) It's shaping up, it's evolving."<br>"(...) Just like all over the world and in Brazil, design is gradually expanding, I think." |
| | | Influence of organizational culture on the role | L 1496-1499-13<br>L 1562-1563-14 | "(...) It certainly has an influence, either for the good or for the bad. To the extent, for example, that everyone starts talking about design thinking, changing the way projects are conceived, this has a total impact on the way you work, you'll work better, more agile, etc. Or not, or it regresses, if you say you're going to work alone and so on..."<br>"(...) Then comes the question of organizational culture, right? Ah, it's always been like this, it's how we work..." |
| | Difficulties faced | Regarding the conceptualization of design and designer | L 1040-12<br>L 529-530 -15 | "(...) I always get confused if I have to explain it to someone who's never heard of it, especially if I'm talking about the web..."<br>"(...) And then who will respect you when you say you're a designer? Then, if they ask you what you are, you can't even answer directly." |
| | | Regarding the definition of Objectivity and Subjectivity and their relationship to art | L 474 -12<br>L 1144-1145-14 | "(...) Art is totally subjective and design isn't always..."<br>"(...) Mainly because of this confusion, I think it affects the arts, I think the guy is an artist, someone with difficult behavior." L 1144-1145 -14 |
| | | Communication and access to information | L 503-504 -16<br>L 524 -17 | "(...) It's even a question, I'm going to make a beautiful, wonderful layout, but I can't find the information..."<br>"(...) Lack of communication..." |
| | | Regarding autonomy at work | L 519-521 -I2<br>L 1510-1512 -12 | "(...) Yes, there are problems with the execution too, you (designer) do it one way and then it's not as you designed it because someone decided to mess with your work..."<br>"(...) How many times do we do something, like the guy from (xxxxxx) who goes there and they do it their way, then he overwrites a file, then he comes back, solves a problem that we didn't solve and they don't even tell us." |
| | | Regarding training, educational, academic, curricular | L 538-539 -15<br>L 555-556 -16 | "(...) College isn't prepared to train you as a professional, really..."<br>"(...) the market needs a professional and so the colleges speed up to fill this space." |
| | | Difficulties specific to the organization | L 691-692-H<br>L 1527-1529- | "(...) I think that basically all the problems come from that story, that everything changes every four |

| | | studied | 17 | years."<br>"(...) People, I think the IT company has the highest average age in the world. There are people who left a brick factory and came here and still make bricks, you know? They've never updated." |
| | | Regarding the lack of regulation of the profession | L 542 -12<br>L 544 -15 | "(...) One problem is that we're not regulated..."<br>"(...) It's another very specific situation. Our profession isn't even regulated." |
| | Credibility of the design profession | | L 593-595 -17<br>L 1407-1411 -13 | "(...) Soon they'll start to realize its importance, which is why I prefer to be called an information architect rather than a designer, I call myself an information architect, because I see myself working with it more. "<br>"(...) Am I proud of my profession? Absolutely. I'm disregarding from this answer the financial issue and the local Brazilian issue, like "ah, Lúcio, but can this be done in Brazil?", yes, but it's what he said, it's how little is invested in research and development, but it doesn't mean that the person has to work here, they can work outside of here, be a designer somewhere else." |
| Skills | Techniques | | L 395 -17<br>L 317 - 318 -13 | "(...) planning, and secondly research."<br>"(...) There's no point in wanting to design good things for people and not knowing anything about the support, the materials, the latest techniques..." |
| | | | L 1268-1269-17 | "(...) Technology helps design, as soon as you upgrade technology, design goes along with it, design sometimes forces technology to move." |
| | Non-technical | Individuals | L 281-284-И<br>L 370-371 -13<br>L 402-404-I7<br>L 440-441 -14 | "(...) So, I think that before the tool you have to be creative, have good taste and study, right? You have to go back and see what's going on. The main thing, I think, is creativity and good taste. In short."<br>"(...) It's basically having an open mind, the ability to synthesize."<br>"(...) a principle that was very good, very practical, which was Simplicity. So anything is easy when it's simple..."<br>"(...) This question of thinking about the project, as a designer, this process is intuitive." |
| | | Social | L 291-297-13 | "(...) The designer has to take part in the initial meetings with the business analyst, understand the problem with the client, talk to the systems team, with the analyst, he always has to be with the team." |

| | | | | L 821-824-17 | "(...) Until recently we saw that most designers didn't know how to manage tension. As they say in medicine, emeraldite syndrome, everyone wanting to be better, to be a star, and they beat each other up and so on..." |
| | | | | L 894-895 -13 | "(...) If a team is managed, well managed, at first there's no such thing... I mean, there may be a discussion about objectives, but it's resolved." |
| | | | | L 874 -16 | "(...) Humble, tolerant and communicative, I think that's it." |

## 4.3.2 Profile of focus group participants - Designers

Before starting to describe the content, it is worth presenting the profile of the participants in the focus group technique. The participants were classified as follows:

**Informant 1** - Male, 52 years old, graduated with a bachelor's degree in social communication - publicity and advertising, employee of PROCERGS as a designer since 1995.

**Informant 2** - Female, 23 years old, Design graduate, design trainee at PROCERGS since 2013.

**Informant 3** - Male, 30 years old, graduated in Design, PROCERGS employee since 2013, but working as a designer since 2001.

**Informant 4** - Male, 38 years old, graduated in Plastic Arts, PROCERGS employee as a designer since 2002.

**Informant 5** - Female, 26 years old, studying design since 2009, design trainee at PROCERGS since 2013.

**Informant 6** - Female, 20 years old, studying design since 2009, design trainee at PROCERGS since 2013.

**Informant 7** - Male, 39 years old, PhD in computer science in education since 2014, PROCERGS employee as a designer since 2000.

## 4.3.3 Description of the focus group content analysis framework - Designers

Following the division into themes, which brought together categories and subcategories of content analysis, the following is a description of what was found in each category and subcategory to be most relevant in relation to the theme and objectives of the research.

Theme: **Papers**

Category: **Assignments**

This category brought together the units of analysis related to the designers' understanding of their duties as designers within the organization. In this way, it sought to identify in the statements of the informants, the different attributions that these professionals considered to be proper to their profession. It was therefore subdivided into the following subcategories:

Subcategory: **Regarding the appearance/presentation of a product/service**

This category of analysis presented units that referred to the designer's role as designing, developing, creating the appearance of a product/service. When asked about the duties of a designer, most of the time during the focus group technique, the designers agreed with the idea that the visual appearance/presentation of a product is a natural attribute of their profession as a designer. An example is the following unit: *"(...) He's the guy who designs to communicate something in graphic form, some need, who is concerned with the appearance, the shape of the product and how it should look to delight its user."* (L1061-1062-I6), or *"(...) So the designer's work is always thought of as visual only..."* (L487-I5).

Subcategory: **Problem-solving attributions**

This category brought together units of analysis whose content included references to problem-solving as being the designer's responsibility. This was clearly discussed during the focus group and there was agreement on the subject among the participants. According to the units analyzed, in addition to just solving problems, the designers stated that this problem-solving follows the designer's specific methods and techniques, as shown in the following unit: "(...) *We develop options for problems using methods specific to the area, and tools and technical knowledge specific to the area."* (L1091-1092-I2).

Subcategory: **Attributions for improving user experience and people's lives**

This category brought together units of analysis in which speakers referred to improving people's experience with products/services, and consequently their lives in a broader sense, as being the designer's responsibility. This can be seen from the first unit selected: "(...) *Improving the experience that users have with products..."* (L1022-I7), which focused solely on people's interaction with products, to more complex statements such as: "(...)[a] *Making people carry out their tasks lightly and with a good experience."* (L1017-1018-I3).

Subcategory: **Attributions regarding the functionality and usability of products**

In this subcategory of analysis, the company's designers clearly see it as their responsibility to make the solutions they develop more functional and easier for people (users) to use, as the following unit shows: "(...) *Thinking of PROCERGS and the government, the best thing for us, as designers here, would be for someone to say something like, "Gee, I had to pay my fine there. Man, that's easy. I took my cell phone here, gave it three taps, I received it at home, great!" That would be the pinnacle!"* (L1026-1029-I3).

Subcategory: **Multidisciplinary roles**

This category brought together the units of analysis that referred to multidisciplinarity or interdisciplinarity, i.e. that pointed to the relationship with different areas of knowledge as an aspect attributed to the activity of design and its professional designers. They therefore presented units such as the one below: "(...) *A person who is connected to different aspects, different knowledge, trends who suddenly finds it easy to create connections between things.* " (L1063-1064 - I5).

Category: **Paper change dynamics**

This category brought together the units of analysis related to the understanding that the designers of the company under investigation have of the mobility of the designer's role within the organization over time. It also sought to identify organizational culture factors cited by the informants that influence this dynamic. It was thus subdivided into the following subcategories:

Subcategory: **Dynamism of the designer's role**

This subcategory brought together the units of analysis that referred to the designer's perception of the movement or dynamics of their role within the organization. Specifically, it sought to understand whether designers had any perception of the question of whether their role within the organization is static, always the same, or whether it is dynamic and can expand and shift. This brought together references such as the following unit, when the informant was asked what he thought about the mobility of the designer's role: (...) *It's shaping up, it's evolving."* (L 578 - I1) where the informant states that he sees this role changing over time, and goes further by saying that this movement is in the sense of evolution.

Subcategory: **Influence of organizational culture on the role**

This subcategory brought together units of analysis that explained the influence of aspects of the organizational culture that influence the role of the designer and, consequently, their dynamics within the organization. When asked about the influence of the organization's culture on the designer's role within the company, a culture made up of its habits, formal and informal rules, standards and methods, the designers agreed that yes, this culture does influence their work and, consequently, their role, as the following unit shows: "(...) *it certainly does, for better or worse. To the extent, for example, that everyone starts talking about design thinking, changing the way projects are conceived, this has a total impact on the way you work, you'll work better, more agile, etc. Or you don't, or you go back, if you say you're going to work alone and so on...*" (L 1496-1499 - I3).

Category: **Difficulties faced by designers**

In order to reflect more broadly on the role of the designer, it was considered important to analyze the difficulties faced by designers in carrying out their professional activity. To this end, this category of analysis brought together subcategories with units of analysis that referred to any and all difficulties the designers encountered in carrying out their work, in the teams and in the organization studied as a whole. As such, and due to the diverse nature of the difficulties reported during the focus group, this category was subdivided into the following subcategories:

Subcategory: **Conceptualization of design and designer**

This subcategory of analysis included units that pointed to the difficulty of correctly conceptualizing the terms design and designer as a difficulty faced by designers in the practical performance of their activity, and in professional relationships with other individuals. Units such as: "(...) *I always get confused if I have to explain it to someone who has never heard of it, especially if I'm talking about the web area...*" were selected. (L 1040 - I2), or "(...) *and then who will respect you when you say you're a designer? Then, if they ask you what you are, they can't even answer properly.*" (L 529-530 - I5).

Subcategory: **Relationship with art and definition of objectivity, Subjectivity of the activity**

This subcategory of analysis included the units of analysis that referred to the relationship between design activity and art, and the confusion between objectivity and subjectivity in design activity. This relationship was a frequent affirmation during the focus group, and was always pointed out by the designers as a difficulty to be faced. So this subcategory brought together units such as: "(...) *Art is totally subjective and design isn't always...*" (L 474 - I2), "(...) we *get mistaken for artists, like "oh, this one is our artist and all, he does beautiful layouts.*" (L 483-484 - I7).

**Subcategory: Communication and access to information**

This subcategory of analysis brought together units present in the designers' speeches which expressed difficulties relating to communication and access to information, as is clear from the following units: "(...) *It's even a question, I'm going to make a beautiful, wonderful layout, but I can't find the information...*" (L503-504 - I6).

Subcategory: **Regarding autonomy at work**

This subcategory presented units of analysis with arguments referring to the designer's lack of autonomy in carrying out his activity within the organization. This difficulty was evident in the selected units:"(...) *Yes, there are problems with execution too, you (designer) do it one way and then it's not as you designed it because someone decided to mess with your work...*" (L519-521 - I2).

Subcategory: **Regarding educational, academic and curricular training**

This subcategory brought together units of analysis that referred to the educational, academic, curricular and cultural training difficulties faced by the designers investigated in the focus group. The findings present in the selected units of analysis denote this difficulty, as the following units show: "(...) *the university isn't prepared to train you as a professional, really...*" (L538-539 - I5), or "(...) *the market needs a professional and so colleges speed up to fill this space.*" (L555-556 - I6).

Subcategory: **Difficulties peculiar to the organization studied**

This subcategory brought together the units of analysis that were specific to the nature of the organization studied, in this case, a public information technology company, as reported by the informants in the focus group. These specific difficulties are described in units such as: "(...) *I think that basically all the problems come from that story, every 4 years everything changes.*" (L691-692 - I1 ).

Subcategory: **Lack of regulation of the profession**

This subcategory grouped together the units of analysis that mentioned problems faced by designers as a result of the lack of regulation of the profession. This brought together units such as: "(...) *One problem is the fact that we are not regulated...*" (L542 - I2), or "(...) *It's another very specific situation. Our profession isn't even regulated.*" (L544 - I5) where the problem of the lack of regulation is mentioned, although "how" this difficulty actually influences the performance of the profession was not made clear by the informants.

Category: **Credibility of the design profession**

This category brought together the units of analysis referring to the credibility of the design profession as perceived by the designers themselves, in other words, the self-image that these professionals have of the professional activity they have chosen. Two units of analysis stand out which illustrate the level of credibility of the profession as perceived by the designers: "(...) *Am I proud of the profession? Absolutely. I'm disregarding from this answer the financial issue and the local Brazilian issue, like "oh, buddy, but can this be done in Brazil?" yes, but it's what he said, how little is invested in research and development, but it doesn't mean that the person has to work here, they can work outside of here, be a designer somewhere else.*" (L 1407-1411 - I3).

**Theme: Skills**

In this research, it is understood that in order to perform a certain role, designers need to mobilize different competencies specific to their activity. In this sense, this theme brought together the categories and subcategories that contained units of analysis that referred to competencies considered important by the informants for working as a designer. As different types of competences emerged, it was more appropriate to make a more specific classification which gave rise to the following categories according to the nature of the competence:

Category: **Technical skills**

This subcategory brought together the most significant units of analysis mentioned in the focus group technique, which were related or referred to the use of methods, techniques and tools that would be considered to be the designer's own and/or also related to new communication and computer technologies as necessary skills to work as a designer in the context observed. In this sense, units such as: "(...) *You have to know how to research, where to look for this information.*" emerged. (L 297-298 - I3) , "(...) *And of course, in addition to parallel things, constant updating, knowledge in his professional area...*" (L 308-309 - I3) and "(...) *planning, and secondly research.*" (L 395 - I7).

Category: **Individual Non-Technical Skills**

Still on the subject of competences, it was considered important to bring together in a subcategory all the units of analysis that referred to individual non-technical competences that a designer should possess in order to work as such. Individual competences, understood here as non-technical skills, but rather psychological, cognitive and personality skills, and which were not related to others or relationships, would be dealt with in the category of social competences. Thus, units of analysis referring to characteristics such as creativity were grouped in this category: "(...) *So, I think that before the tool you have to have creativity, good taste and study, right? You have to look to see what's going on. I think the main thing is creativity and good taste. In short.*" (L 281-284 - I1), or "(...) *And you always have to learn... always be willing to learn*" (L 886 - I1).

The ability to synthesize was also mentioned several times as an important skill for designers, not least because they deal with situations that involve several variables and a high level of complexity, as the following units show: "(...) *Basically it's having an open mind, the ability to synthesize.*" (L 370-371 - I3). Another important attribute as an individual competence that was mentioned in the focus group was simplicity, as the following unit makes clear: "(...) *a principle that was very good, very practical, which was simplicity. So anything is easy when it's simple...*" (L 402-404 - I7).

Other virtues that a designer needs to develop as social skills were also mentioned, such as "(...) *Modesty. I can sum it up like this: modesty. In everything.*" (L 863 - I1), patience, which was mentioned directly: "(...) *Patience!*" (L 868 - I2). The relationship with culture was also cited as an attribute to be developed as a competence for a designer, as appears in the following unit: "(...) *A person who is connected to culture, a person who is in tune*" (L 1071 - I5) or in "(...) *This question of thinking about the project, as a designer, this process is intuitive.*" (L 440-441 - I4) and "(...) *Working with intuitive processes, synthesizing the context of all this and at the same time thinking about who is going to receive this solution that design is trying to offer. The process of intuition is the most interesting, various interfaces of design, such as the arts, architecture, and we try to make a synthesis that meets solutions.*" (L 323-327 - I4).

Category: **Social Non-Technical Skills**

Since this research focused on designers working in multidisciplinary teams, and what their role and competences would be in this context, relationships with other individuals were considered important. In this sense, this category of analysis brought together the units that referred to social skills, which were considered relationship skills that the designers investigated pointed out as necessary skills for the practice of design in the context of the teams and the organization studied, which is clear from units such as: "(...) *The designer has to take part in the initial meetings with the business analyst, understand the problem with the client, talk to the systems team, with the analyst, he always has to be with the team.*" (L 793-795 - I3), "(...) *There again, the skills. The ability to work in a team. It seems to me that it's always been very obvious that we're better able to work with people from other teams...*" (L 812-817 - I7).

Other units made explicit the need to deal with and manage the tensions and conflicts that arise in team relationships, as being important social skills in design practice, as the following units show: "(...) *Until recently we saw that designers, for the most part, didn't know how to manage tensions. As they say in medicine, emeraldite syndrome, everyone wanting to be the best, to be a star and to beat each other up and so on (...) (L 821-824 - I7),* or in *"(...) when you work in a team there are conflicts. There are conflicts, there always will be, there are different perceptions..."* (L 882-883 - I7).

This concludes this first presentation of results with a description of the tables, categories, subcategories and units of analysis selected. Next is a description of the interviews with non-designers. After this description, the units of analysis will be interpreted in the discussion based on the objectives and theoretical framework of this research.

4.4 CATEGORIES OF ANALYSIS - NON-DESIGNERS (SEMI-STRUCTURED IN-DEPTH INTERVIEWS)

For the content analysis of the transcripts of the interviews with the non-designers, we also tried to use Nigel Cross's study (1984) as a basis, in order to define some a priori categories to classify the units of analysis that were related to the objectives of this research. However, as well as being insufficient to explain the relationships in the context studied due to the fact that the work had different objectives and was being carried out in a different context, we were now dealing with non-designers reporting their opinions and describing their image of the designer and how they related to this professional.

After reading the transcribed material, this change in the target audience meant that new categories had to be created. These categories were not only different from Cross's (1984) work, which sought other, more superficial research objectives for the construction of an article, but also different, in part, from the categories already defined in this research for the content analysis of the focus group held with the designers.

This time we were dealing with non-designers giving their opinions on the role of designers and their relationship with these professionals in multidisciplinary teams. As such, the categories of analysis needed to be more in line with the objectives of the research, relating to the expectations of non-designers, not the motivations that led them to the profession or the difficulties of working as a designer, since they couldn't talk about this because they weren't designers. It was necessary to understand the role and skills of the designer through the image that non-designers had of the profession and its agents.

In the case of non-designers, the need for content analysis to focus on the image non-designers have of this professional, their expectations of this professional's work, and their role and competencies in this area was much more evident.

A greater focus on relationships and social skills was also sought, given that, in an information technology company that operates through multidisciplinary teams that meet demands and which is mostly made up of professionals from the exact sciences such as computing, the designer is the type of professional who stands out from the rest, which is proven when we talk about a total of 9 designers in a spectrum of 1200 employees of the company studied.

### 4.4.1 Profile of Interviewees - Non-Designers

This section presents the profile of the non-designers who took part in the semi-structured in-depth interviews and describes the categories and respective units of analysis selected because they were deemed significant in relation to the objectives of this research.

Before beginning the presentation and description of the content analysis tables, it is convenient to present a description of the profile of each NON-DESIGNER informant who was selected and interviewed in this research, as was planned in the method chapter. Thus, the participants were classified as follows:

**Informant 1** - Female, 38 years old, Master Systems Analyst, graduated in Systems Analysis, employee of the company for 16 years, currently in the position of manager of the DDS solutions development division. She manages the division with designers and non-designers.

**Informant 2** - Female, 40 years old, Master Systems Analyst, graduated in Systems Analysis, employee of the company for 16 years, currently in the position of head of the web services sector - SSW (a sector which brings together 77% of the company's designers) belonging to the DDS solutions division. She manages the sector with designers and non-designers.

**Informant 3** - Male, 55 years old, with a degree in Physics, a postgraduate degree in Information Systems and Marketing, an employee of the company for 34 years, currently in the position of Business Analyst in the company's commercial sector. He is part of teams of designers and non-designers and serves clients.

**Informant 4** - Female, 38 years old, graduate with a postgraduate degree in Systems Analysis, Employee of the company for 17 years, currently in the position of Systems Analyst for web projects. She is part of teams with designers and non-designers.

**Informant 5** - Male, 52 years old, computer technician and Systems Analysis graduate, company employee for 16 years, currently Systems Analyst for web projects. He is part of teams with designers and non-designers.

**Informant 6** - Male, 22 years old, studying Information Systems, employee of the company for 4 months, currently working as a web programmer. He is part of teams with designers and non-designers.

**Informant 7** - Female, 42 years old, graduated in Administration, post-graduate in Marketing and Management, employee of the company for 16 years, currently in the position of business analyst in the commercial sector of the company. She is part of a team of designers and non-designers, and serves clients.

## 4.2 Table of Contents Analysis - In-Depth Interviews - Non-Designers

Table 4 - Table of categories, subcategories and units of content analysis applied to the transcription of interviews with non-designers

| "ma | Categories | Sub-categories | LinhaZInformante | Units of Analysis |
|---|---|---|---|---|
| 3peis | Duties | **How much appearance/presentation of a product/service** | L279-281 -12<br>L1228-1229 -15<br>L2360-2362 -17 | "(...) The designer is the one who extracts what is interesting and presents it in a simple and beautiful way, from there the project begins, the work..."<br>"(...) I'm not even going to get into the subject of shapes, colors, details and styles, because that's their business..."<br>"(...) The role of the designer here, as I see it, would be the graphic interface, the part of visual and graphic art, conceptualizing for the whole question of websites that we develop and systems." |
| | | **As for visual thinking, giving shape to ideas** | L390-391 -I2<br>L1504-1505 - I5 | "(...) it may not even be a draft, but it's a drawing of a process, it's a sketch, an image, something visual, you know, that makes it easier to understand."<br>"(...) he has a more visual reasoning, more refined, he can give form to ideas, which we have difficulty with..." |
| | | **Improving people's experiences and lives** | L60-I1<br>L1518-1522-I5 | "(...) This role is fundamental, to simplify things, people's lives."<br>"(...) The designer is the guy who says, I don't just need this, I have to have a screen that tells me what the traffic car looks like, what the traffic car looks like, I have to have a seat that hugs me better, I have to perfect it, make people's lives easier, I have to try to interpret and improve every aspect to make things better and better, more suited to what users need." |
| | | **In terms of meeting the specific needs of users/clients** | L35-36-I1 | "(...) So I think it fits into one of the important roles, very important for software development, to achieve the goal, which is customer and user satisfaction." |
| | | | L283-284 -12 | "(...) You have to see the role of the user, the client |

| | | | | |
|---|---|---|---|---|
| | | | | and the developer. Put yourself in their shoes." |
| | | **Regarding the functionality and usability of the products** | L23-24-I1<br>L496-499 -I3<br>L1670-1671 -I5 | "(...) That I can use, that it's easy and useful, he (the designer) has a fundamental role..."<br>"(...) Today there's a whole concept of dynamics, and interpretation, of access, of ease of recognition, of the study of colors, of use, of how you can make people pay attention, you can make that situation pass in front of another situation. I mean, that's what a designer does."<br>(...) Anyway, you can do a lot of things, right, so thanks to whom? Thanks to the designers who think not only about the appearance but also the functionality of things! |
| | | **Multidisciplinarity** | L20-22-I1<br>L894-898 -I4 | (...) Because the designer has several, let's say, applications. But within software development, in our context here at PROCERGS, I see the designer as an important part when we need several fronts, to connect different areas..."<br>"(...) And also to be that person who suddenly manages to give that idea not seen in the work, manages to complement the team in a multidisciplinary way, to connect and communicate with different areas, I think that in this part of web projects especially, this is fundamental and this is what the designer does." |
| | | **When it comes to interpreting complex contexts** | L73-74-I1<br>L277-279 -I2<br>L1311-1312 -I5 | "(...) The ability to grasp, interpret, understand a target audience, a situation full of variables..."<br>"(...) It's in the designer's nature to interpret all the confusing information that sometimes happens in a meeting and nobody knows what they want."<br>"(...) The designer has the role, I see it first as the pathfinder, of understanding what the problem is to be solved in the midst of the client's mess." |
| | | **Subjectivity and objectivity and the relationship to art** | L182-185 - I1 | "(...) What strikes me most is the artistic side, precisely because I'm from the other side, the Cartesian side. For me, looking at the designer, it's the guy who's an artist, who knows how to translate, how to make a drawing, how to translate a feeling, a client's desire..." |
| | | | L609-610-I3<br>L2311-2312-I7 | "(...) It's in that sense, and that's the designer's expertise, to add art in these tougher, more precise contexts."<br>"(...) Because design is creation, right, and sometimes a creation is almost a work of art, right?" |

| | | | | |
|---|---|---|---|---|
| | | Mediator assignment | L544-546 -13<br>L1488-1489 -15 | "(...) Intermediary I think, I think that would be the best word, intermediary. Between the data and the information, between the source and the destination, you know? I'd be in the middle "..." in that middle ground."<br>"(...) He's an interpreter, he's in the middle helping to translate needs, he's a mediator really..." |
| | Role dynamics in the organization | The dynamic role of the designer | L233-236-I1<br>L2386-2388 -17 | "(...) I think their role and performance in the company can change, has already changed, I think so. The information architect himself, I think so, things are changing."<br>"(...) I don't think it's more widespread because of the lack of publicity. If no one talks and communicates with people, it's more difficult to understand because it's a different profession to most people here." |
| | | Cultural influence<br>Organizational on paper | L218-221 -11<br>L1049-1051 -I4 | "(...) I think so, the company limits us in the sense that we try to standardize some things in order to be productive, so maybe that does limit us."<br>"(...) I think that the culture of the company does have a bit of an influence, because we have those ways of working, patterns, methods, rules and even hierarchy, right, and all this slows down the designer a bit." |
| Difficulties faced when working with designers | | | L2492-2494 -17<br>L1453-1454-I5 | "(...) And that's another problem I've also had, which is a question of time, so I've never been able to schedule a meeting in the morning because then they go on their trips, so in the morning they're always introspective, and I've noticed..."<br>"(...) Sometimes a big ego is like a big eye, it harms the group, it's a difficulty to deal with when you're in teams." |
| Image of the professional designer | Designer look | | L196-198 -11 | "(...) There are some who are more alternative in the way they dress, I guess, but... They're more open-minded, they're not classic, they're more alternative, I'd say, in day-to-day life. In the way they dress, but also in the way they speak, communicate..." |
| | | | L1551-1553 -15 | "(...) A long time ago, designers had to wear red sneakers, plaid pants, a green jacket, half a mask (laughs), a little corn, and an elaborate beard, but today that stereotype no longer exists." |
| | | The importance of the designer | L839-840 -13<br>L1483-1484 -I5 | "(...) So how does the organization see designers? It sees them as a necessity."<br>"(...) I can't imagine working on a project without a designer, there's no project." |
| | | Similar | L102-104 - 11 | "(...) I think that all this part that has Creativity with an |

| | | | | |
|---|---|---|---|---|
| | | professions | | advertising company, I don't know if journalism, a company that works with the media, presenting to people, interacting with people... I think it has this footprint..." |
| | | | L615-616-I3 | "(...) Architecture I think has something to do with it, engineering I think has a lot to do with it.... professions that depend on technical creativity." |
| | | | L1266-1267-I5 | "(...) Which has to do with corn design, I see it's motorsport, right, motorsport is interesting because it's the designers who are going to create the cars, right..." |
| | | Different professions | L312-313-I2 L935-937 -14 L1292-I5 | "(...) Totally different? (Laughs) Medicine, for example, would be something like that? Yeah, something more health-oriented? Or any other area, or even ex-pat." "(...) Accountants. These very systematic professions, banking, these very closed things. Auditors, you have to follow the law, there's no flexibility. I think that's the way I see it." "(...) Analysis of a more precise, more closed, more inflexible system. |
| Skills | Techniques | | L70-72-I1 | "(...) And there's also this very technical part of not making it heavy, I think you have to know a lot about system development, and the user, right, how they think to navigate, the layout of the navigation, you have to know it well to help set up the interfaces." |
| | | | L1243-1245 -I5 | "(...) Secondly, I think you have to study to work with corn design, to know the process, the tools, the way to approach problems..." |
| Non-technical | Individuals | L65-69-I1 L288-289 -12 L412-413-12 L1500-1503 - I5 | | "(...) I think there's the Creativity part, normally developers are very Cartesian, very square, and designers have this creative side. I think that if you're not creative, you can't do it. You have to be able to imagine the colors, understand the client and be able to reproduce a brand, a design, you have to have a lot of creativity." "(...) She has to have a critical sense to discuss the idea, have a good power of argument, she has to be creative..." "(...) This power to synthesize, to filter." "(...) The designer is... in 99% of cases he has good taste, so that's a great skill that a person needs to have to work as a designer, good taste, a good reference and experience." |
| | Social | L137-141 -I1 | | "(...) Willing to share what you know and receive criticism or suggestions, without seeing it as negative criticism, I think that's how teamwork works... you think about the success of the whole, not the individual. There's no point in me doing my |

| | | | | |
|---|---|---|---|---|
| | | L971-976-I4 | | bit if the others can't do theirs, we've lost the game, there's no point in me just doing my bit. " "(...) I think it's very important to exchange information, communication, that idea that it's not my job, it's our job. If we make a mistake, we make a mistake, it's not you who's wrong and that thing about everyone feeling responsible. If we're working on this project and we have this deadline, I'm not the one who has to demand it, everyone has to work together, this awareness. I think the team has to |
| | | L2468-2471 -17 | | be a team..." "(...) It's again this question of accepting change, accepting criticism, knowing how to accept the question of resilience, because then you come back and I think it's much more important is the role of the team leader there, he doesn't let the Little Sheep have that leadership and doesn't let any sheep go astray." |

## 4.4.3 Description of the content analysis framework for in-depth interviews - Non-Designers

Following the division into themes, which bring together categories and subcategories of content analysis, the following is a description of the units of analysis selected as relevant in relation to the theme and objectives of the research.

Theme: **Papers**

Category - **Designer duties**

This category brought together the units of analysis related to the understanding that the non-designers of the company under investigation have of what the designers' duties are within the organization. It was then subdivided into the following subcategories:

Subcategory - **Regarding the appearance/presentation of a product/service**

This category of analysis presented units that referred to the designer's role as designing, developing, creating the appearance of a product/service. The majority of interviewees agreed with the idea that the visual appearance/presentation of a product/service is a natural attribute of the design activity. This attribution is clear in the units that refer to the beauty, the look, the appearance, the aesthetics of the product/service, as the following units show: "(...) *The designer is the one who extracts what is interesting and presents it in a simple and beautiful way, from there the project, the work begins.*" (L279-281 - I2), or "(...) *The role of the designer here and as I see it would be the graphic interface, the visual and graphic art part, conceptualizing for the whole issue of websites that we develop and systems.*" (L2360-2362 - I7).

Subcategory - **Visual thinking, shaping ideas**

This subcategory brought together the units of analysis that referred to the designer's natural attribute as visual reasoning, the ability to shape ideas, mainly through their imagination and drawing skills.

An example of a unit from this subcategory is the following unit: "(...) it *may not even be a sketch, but there's a drawing of a process, there's a sketch, an image, something visual, you know, that makes it easier to understand". (L390-391 - I2)*, or in "(...) *he has a more visual, more refined way of thinking, he manages to give shape to ideas, which we find difficult...* " (L1504-1505 - I5).

Subcategory - **Improving people's experience and lives**

This subcategory of analysis brought together the units that presented aspects related to improving people's experience when interacting with products/services by facilitating and simplifying tasks and, consequently, improving people's lives.

Some units were clear in pointing out this attribution, such as the one below: "(...) *This role is fundamental, to simplify things, people's lives.*" (L60- I1).

Subcategory - Meeting **the specific needs of users/clients**

This subcategory brought together the units of analysis referring to meeting needs and satisfying the user client was mentioned in the following unit: "(...) *So I think it fits into one of the important roles, very important for software development, to achieve the goal, which is customer and user satisfaction."* (L35-36 - I1), or in: "(...) *You have to understand what the client wants and what the users want.*" (L2517 - I7).

**Subcategory - Product functionality and usability**

These two very close concepts appeared frequently in the units of analysis as one of the most frequent concerns attributed to designers, as the following unit shows: (...) *well, you can do a lot of things, right, so thanks to whom? Thanks to the designers who think not only about the appearance but the functionality of things!"* (L1670-1671 - I5). Making things easier, more attractive and easier to use was sometimes chosen by the informants as the main function of the designer, as the following unit shows: "(...) *That he can use it, that it's easy and useful, he (the designer) has a fundamental role (...)"* (L23-24 - I1 ).

Subcategory - **Multidisciplinarity**

This subcategory brought together the units of analysis that referred to the attribute of multidisciplinarity as also being characteristic of the activity of design and its practitioner, which was also sometimes defined as the ability to connect different areas and knowledge. In this sense, the following units were selected: "(...) *Because a designer has several, shall we say, applications. But within software development, in our context here at PROCERGS, I see the designer as an important part when we need several fronts,*

*connecting different areas..."* (L20-22 - I1) and also the following: "(...) *And also to be that person who suddenly manages to give that idea not only in the work, manages to complement the team in a multidisciplinary way, to connect and communicate with different areas, I think that in this part of web projects especially this is fundamental and this is what the designer does."* (L894-898 - I4), where this attribution is made explicit.

Subcategory - **Interpreting complex contexts**

This subcategory also didn't exist in the content analysis of the focus group with designers, however, when analyzing the transcripts of the interviews, it was noticed that among non-designers, this task of deciphering contexts influenced by various variables, known and unknown, was one of the most frequently cited tasks, as being the designer's own, often justifying the designer's participation in projects, from the first contact with the client. This brought together units such as the following: "(...) The *ability to grasp, interpret, understand a target audience, a situation full of variables."* (L73- 74 - I1), "(...) *It's part of the designer's nature to interpret all the confusing information that sometimes happens in a meeting and nobody knows what they want."* (L277- 279 - I2).

Subcategory - **The designer's relationship with art** (objectivity and subjectivity)

This subcategory brought together the units of analysis that contained references to the relationship between design activity and art, perceived by non-designers as an important attribute and even a differentiating factor for designers compared to other professionals.

This relationship, which in itself implies a different way of looking at problems, was often cited in the statements of the informants as a natural talent that they, non-designers, did not possess, as the following units show: "(...) *That, the question of art is a differentiator for the designer."* (L114 - I1) or in: "*What strikes me most is the artistic side, precisely because I'm from the other side, the Cartesian side. For me, looking at the designer, it's the guy who's an artist, who knows how to translate, how to make a drawing, how to translate a feeling, a client's desire (...)"* (L182-185 - I1).

Subcategory - **Regarding the role of mediator**

This subcategory brought together the units of analysis that referred to the role of mediator, or intermediary between different realities, as being an attribute proper to designers and their activity. This is evident in the following unit: *"(...) Intermediator I think, I think that would be the best word, intermediator. Between the data and the information, between the source and the destination, you know? He would be in the middle "..." in that middle ground."* (L544-546 - I3).

Category: **Paper change dynamics**

This category brought together the units of analysis related to the understanding that non-designers in the company under investigation have of the mobility of the designer's role within the organization over time. This category also sought to identify organizational culture factors, mentioned by the informants, which influence this dynamic. It was therefore subdivided into the following subcategories:

Subcategory: **Dynamicity of the design role**

This subcategory brought together the units of analysis that referred to non-designers' perceptions of the changing or dynamic role of the designer within the organization. Specifically, it sought to understand whether non-designers had any perception of whether the role of the designer within the company is static (always the same) or dynamic and can expand and shift over time and in the different areas of a company. In this way, he came up with units such as: *"(...) I think their role and performance in the company can change, has already changed, I think so. The information architect himself, I think so, things are changing."* (L233-236 - I1).

Subcategory - **Influence of organizational culture on the role of the designer**

This subcategory brought together units of analysis that explained the influence of organizational culture on the role of the designer and, consequently, on its dynamics (expansion, retraction or stability) within the organization. When asked about the influence of the organization's culture on the designer's role within the company, the non-designers agreed that yes, this culture does influence their work and, consequently, their role, as the following units show: *"(...) I think so, the company limits us in the sense that we try to standardize some things in order to be productive, so maybe it does."* (L218- 221 - I1), or even in: *"(...) I think the company culture does have a bit of an influence, not least because we have those ways of working, standards, methods, rules and even hierarchy, right, and all of this puts a bit of a brake on the designer"* (L1049-1051 - I4).

Category - **Difficulties faced when working with designers**

This category of analysis sought to bring together the speech units of the non-designer interviewees where reference was made to problems faced when working with designers.

The difference in temperaments and the difficulties arising from this difference were evident. Difficulties that directly influenced the role of the designer within the organization, as the following units point out: "(...) *That's it and another problem I've also had, which is a question of time, so I've never been able to schedule a meeting in the morning because then, as they go on their trips, in the morning they're always introspective, and I notice it.*" (L2492-2494 - I7), or in: "(...) *Too big an ego sometimes, a big ego is like a big eye, right, it harms the group, it's a difficulty to deal with when you're in teams.*" (L1453-1454 - I5).

Category - **Professional designer image**

This category of analysis brought together the units that referred to how non-designers perceived the image of the designer. As such, it dealt with statements that referred to aspects relating firstly to the appearance and stereotype of the designer, and secondly to the importance of this professional for the company and for society.

In addition, to complement their understanding of this perceived image, the informants were asked to compare the activity of design and its practitioners with other professions that they thought were similar to or completely different from design. This category was then subdivided into the following two subcategories.

Subcategory - **Designer appearance**

This subcategory brought together the units of analysis that referred to external aspects of a designer's appearance. In this sense, it presented units with speeches that made explicit aspects such as the way of dressing, walking and communicating, perceived by non-designers as the designer's own. Thus, units were selected which made direct reference to style and dress, as can be seen in the following unit: "(...) *There are some who are more alternative in the way they dress, I guess, but... They're more open-minded, they're not classics, they're more alternative, I'd say, on a day-to-day basis. In the way they dress, but also in the way they speak, the way they communicate...*" (L196-198 - I1).

Subcategory - **Importance of the designer**

This subcategory brought together the units of analysis that made some reference to the importance of designers in the company studied and in society in general. This importance was clearly evident in units such as: "(...) *So how does the organization see designers? It sees them as a necessity.*" (L839-840 - I3), or "(...) *I can't imagine working on a project without a designer, it's not a project.*" (L1483-1484 - I5).

Subcategory - **Professions similar to design**

This category brought together the units of analysis which referred to professions which, according to the informants' perceptions, were similar to the designer's profile, whether in terms of their processes, the way professionals work, communicate, appearance or other matters. It's important to note that the professions most often cited as being similar in various aspects were Architecture and Communication, as can be seen in the selected units of analysis: "(...) *Architecture I think has something to do with it, engineering I think has a lot to do with it.... professions that depend on technical creativity.*" (L615-616 - I3), or in "(...) *I think that all this part that has creativity with advertising companies, I don't know if journalism, companies that work with the media, presenting to people, interacting with people... I think it has this footprint...*" (L102-104 - I1).

Subcategory - **Professions other than design**

Following the comparison exercise requested, this subcategory brought together the units of analysis that mentioned activities or professionals considered by the informants to be distinct from design and the designer. It thus brought together units such as: "(...) *Like an accountant, who deals with that there, I think maybe also the developer.*" (L110-I1), or in: "(...) *Totally different? (Laughs) Medicine, for example, would be something like that? Yeah, something more health-oriented? Or something else, or even exact.*" (L312-313 - I2), or comparing it to the non-designer professionals in the organization studied, with systems analyst being the most frequent among employees, as the following unit shows: "(...) *More exact system analysis, more closed, let's say more inflexible.*" (L1292 - I5).

Theme: **Skills**

The categories and subcategories presented in this topic refer to the skills deemed necessary to work as a designer, as perceived and mentioned by the informants during the interviews. In the interviewees' speeches, competences of a different nature were perceived, so it was more appropriate to make a more specific classification which gave rise to the following categories and subcategories according to the nature of the competence:

Category - **Technical Skills**

This category brought together the units of analysis that referred to technical knowledge related to methods, techniques, tools, new communication and computer technologies. It thus brought together units such as: "(...) *And there's also this very technical part of not getting too heavy, I think you have to know a lot about system development, and the user, right, how they think to navigate, the layout of the navigation, you have to know it well to help set up the interfaces."* (L70-72 - I1) or *"(...) Secondly, I think you have to study to work with design, know the process, the tools, the way to approach problems."* (L1243-1245 - I5).

Category - **Individual Non-Technical Skills**

This category of competencies brought together the selected units of analysis that referred to the individual competencies that a designer should possess in order to act as such, as perceived by non-designers. Thus, units of analysis such as: *"(...) This question of creativity, I think it's a priority."* (L888 - I4) were grouped in this subcategory. (L888 - I4) or in: *"(...) I think there's the creativity part, normally developers are very Cartesian, very square, and designers have this creative side. I think that if you're not creative, you can't do it. You have to be able to imagine the colors, understand the client and be able to reproduce a brand, a design, you have to have a lot of creativity. "* (L65-69 - I1).

Category - **Social Non-Technical Skills**

This category brought together the units of analysis relating to relationships with other individuals. In this way, various relationship skills related to sharing information and communication, as can be seen in the following units: *"(...) I think it's very important to exchange information, communication, that idea that it's not my job, it's our job. If we make a mistake, we make a mistake, it's not you who's wrong and that thing about everyone feeling responsible. If we're working on this project and we have this deadline, I'm not the one who has to demand it, everyone has to work together, this awareness. I think the team has to be a team..."* (L971-976 - I4) or in *"(...) It's again this question of accepting change, accepting criticism, knowing how to accept the question of resilience, because then you come back and I think it's much more important is the role of the team leader there, he doesn't let the little sheep have that leadership and doesn't let any sheep go astray."* (L2468- 2471 - I7).

This concludes the chapter presenting the results, which describes the content analysis tables of the transcriptions of the focus group with designers and the in-depth interviews with non-designers. The categories, subcategories and respective units of analysis selected according to their relationship with the objectives of this research and interpreted by the researcher have been described.

The discussion chapter follows, where some of the interpretations will be explored in greater depth and where the results will be compared with the content presented in the theoretical framework.

# 5. DISCUSSION

This section of the dissertation aims to deepen the content analysis carried out with the transcription of the focus group with designers and the in-depth interviews with non-designers in the light of the concepts presented in the theoretical framework, with regard to the roles and competencies of the designer. This in-depth study will therefore cover the following items:

5.1   - On the role and skills (technical, individual and social) of the designer;

5.2   - On human-centered design, user-centered design and interaction design;

5.3   - Difficulties faced by designers in carrying out their work in the context studied;

5.4   - The multiple roles of the designer (presentation of the comparative table of competencies and the summary figure).

## 5.1 ON THE ROLE AND SKILLS OF THE DESIGNER

In the theoretical reference section of this dissertation, authors such as Nigel Cross (1984, 1992, 1995) were presented, and the other by the Swedes Lowgren and Stolterman (1998), Flaviano Celaschi (2000), Brigite Borja de Mozota (2003), Francesco Zurlo (2010) and Rafael Cardoso (2013), who presented sets of competencies and attributions that would be specific to the designer.

Cross argues that designers should be able to:

> (a) producing unexpected stories and solutions; (b) tolerating uncertainty and working with incomplete or ill-defined information and solving ill-defined problems; (c) applying imagination and constructive forethought to practical problems; (d) using non-verbal resources such as: drawings / graphics / media / spatial modeling among other media as means of modeling problem solving; (e) adopting solution-focused strategies; (f) employing abductive thinking; (g) working with several alternative design solutions in parallel in order to understand the problem-solution space. (CROSS 1984, 1992, 1995).

Let's analyze each competence suggested by the author above, relating it to the information collected and built up in this research:

Regarding the competence of (a) producing unexpected stories and solutions, at various points in the speeches, both by designers and non-designers, the ability to serve the client and delight the user was mentioned, through the creation of solutions that aim to "serve", "delight" and even "surprise" clients and users, such as the following unit: "(...) So I think it fits into one of the important roles, very important for software development, to be able to achieve the objective, which is to satisfy the client and the user....] *So I think it fits into one of the important roles, very important for software development, to achieve the goal, which is customer and user satisfaction."* (L35-36 - I1) or *"(...) He's the guy who designs to communicate something graphically, some need, who cares about the appearance, the shape of the product and how it should look to delight its user."* (L1061-1062-I6).

Complementing this view, it can be added that the observation that was made in relation to the company studied, in the sector where the designers are located, allowed us to realize that the moment when the layouts of the interface of a site/system are presented, as happens in the company investigated, is a moment that can be compared to telling a story. This is because at these moments, the information about the context that has been gathered and taken into account for the project is taken into account, the *wireframe is* presented: this can be defined as a structural skeleton of the site/system to be developed and functions as a structural outline of the solution and, based on this structure, a graphical interface proposal is built and presented to the client in the form of site/system screens.

This process of collecting, processing and constructing information and generating solution proposals, which includes the client as a key element from the start, as stated by Stappers, Visser, and Kistemaker (2011), makes the client perceive the solution construction process in its entirety. The client understands the story and the process behind the construction of a solution, which largely eliminates the room for subjectivity, since the choices are validated little by little, and jointly between the development team and the client. In this way, satisfactory solutions are reached more quickly.

Regarding the competence to (b) tolerate uncertainty and work with incomplete or ill-defined information and solve ill-defined problems, it can be said, in view of the material analyzed, reported by designers and non-designers investigated in this research, that it is verified in the practice of design activity.

The designer's ability to unravel the client's mess, or complex contexts influenced by different variables, has been mentioned several times.

On these occasions, the designer was perceived as someone who has the ability to uncover ill-defined contexts, needs that are not even perceived by the clients or users themselves, problems that lack precise definition. However, according to the data analyzed, there seems to be a difference in perception between designers and non-designers on this topic. For non-designers, this special competence for unraveling and interpreting complex contexts influenced by different variables was clearly perceived and cited as one of the designer's differentials, as the following unit shows: *"(...) The designer has the function, I see it as the first pathfinder, of understanding what the problem is to be solved in the midst of the client's mess."* (L1311-1312 - I5). The clear awareness that this is a designer's responsibility also justifies the designer's participation in projects from the first contact with the client.

This responsibility to really understand the problem to be solved is due to a lack of definition in the client's context, or the client's lack of knowledge of the technologies involved in developing the solution. In this way, the designer is given the ability to understand their context and problems even better than the client or user themselves.

However, this competence was much more important in the reports of non-designers. For these professionals, there is a strong notion that this competence is the designer's own, to the extent that it was an analysis category that brought together all the quotes that referred to the competence of interpreting complex contexts, which was always emphasized by the non-designer informants, which is in line with what Stompff (2012) said, when he cited this ability to interpret complexity as being necessary for the designer in the practice of their activity (STOMPFF, 2012).

This ability to analyze and interpret complex contexts and synthesize them with a view to finding a solution is related to the design *capabilities* proposed by Zurlo (where the ability to see is understood as the ability to read contexts and systems in an oriented way). (ZURLO, 2010) is a very basic design capability.

Analyzing each designer's ability in isolation, it is possible to see from the information collected and constructed that the ability to see is verified when the informants affirm the ability to interpret complex contexts and the need for the designer to have a systemic vision, interested not only in the constituent elements of the system, but also in the relationships established between them, which can be verified in the selected units.

Based on this information collected, filtered, hierarchized and the correct observation of relationships and influencing factors, the designer puts into practice his second ability, that of predicting, understood as the ability to critically anticipate the future and uncertainties, and in the midst of such vagueness, to be able to make appropriate and satisfactory choices of solutions to his users' problems. There is a direct relationship between this ability and the question "What if?", which is so present in the practice of designers, as was seen in the statements of the informants and the observation of their context.

So much emphasized by non-designers, this attribute was never mentioned directly or indirectly by designers about their activity. There are three possible reasons for this difference in perception of such a significant competence.

First of all, it may be that designers have never admitted to such a task or perceived it to be necessary to mention it, because admitting to such a broad and difficult task as interpreting complex contexts is, for the designer, like taking on a responsibility that goes beyond their real capabilities and competencies, This could lead to an image of arrogance, as someone who thinks he is more capable than he really is, and therefore very different from the other members of the teams, which could damage his image and professional recognition and put him in complicated situations when these duties and competences are really required.

The second probable reason that could explain this difference in perception is that this ability to interpret complexity is something so natural and intrinsic to the activity that it didn't come up during the focus group.

The third reason for this difference in perception is that the company being investigated develops information technology and Internet solutions, and this subject is still relatively new to most of the public bodies, departments and managers served by the company. This lack of knowledge on the subject on the part of the client also leads to a poor definition of the problem and a poor understanding of the variables involved in the client's context.

Thus, the designer is asked to present a solution proposal that at the same time clarifies the problem and the client's context, since this professional will gather and capture the most important information from the client and their context in order to, based on their creative ability, propose an internet solution that starts with the visual, the interface, where the user will interact with the system.

In any case, based on the research carried out, it is possible to admit that the ability to interpret these complex, ill-defined, imprecise and uncertain contexts is a real ability, and designers are required to mobilize it in the course of their professional activity.

When it comes to websites and systems, technological products made up of functional properties and which are increasingly present in people's daily lives, the designer is given another task, which is to worry about the functionality and usability of the solutions he designs. This is in line with Lowgren and Stolterman's (1998) assertion that the design of functional properties requires insight and knowledge of use. The ability to combine these two concepts was recognized by the survey informants as one of the main duties of a designer in the context studied, as the following unit shows: "(...) *That he can use it, that it's easy and useful, he (the designer) has a fundamental role...*" (L23-24 - I1).

Perceived by designers and non-designers alike as one of the main duties of a designer, the concern and responsibility for the functionality and usability of a product/service and its form (appearance) were combined in several units of analysis from the focus group and the interviews, indicating that there is a clear notion among the informants investigated that the function and usability of a product/service is a duty proper to design and goes hand in hand with aesthetic responsibility.

In order to achieve continuous improvement in the functionality and usability of the solutions developed at the company studied, the designer needs the attribute of perspicacity, understood here as an easy understanding of situations, being a good observer, a person who analyzes things well, who sees things in an intelligent way, above the ordinary level and who finds it easy to solve problems. But as well as being perceptive, designers need to have a deep understanding of how the solutions they develop are used, and to do this they need to have knowledge of usability.

The usability of websites and web systems, solutions where the designer works in the company studied, is a concern seen as the designer's entire responsibility, as the following unit shows: "(...) *Today there's a whole concept of dynamics, and interpretation, of access, of ease of recognition, of studying colors, of use, of how you can make people pay attention, you can make that situation go before another situation. I mean, only a designer can do that.*" (L496-499 - I3)

This perception of the importance of functionality and usability is common among the designers themselves, who develop in-depth knowledge of this issue in their degree courses, but mainly in the practice of their activity, and among non-designers who place on these professionals the responsibility for facilitating the accomplishment of tasks through the study of the usability of products/services. At various points in the informants' speeches, this attribution was placed alongside aesthetic responsibility in terms of importance and was sometimes considered the main concern that a design professional should have in the context studied, as the following unit shows: "(...) *It's just that aesthetics is there for function, you know? I don't think aesthetics are purely aesthetic, because they serve function.*" (L 1252-1253 - I6) where the relationship between aesthetics and function is clear.

Analysis such as this has shown that there is a concern to connect different areas of knowledge and a goal of serving and "enchanting" a user of the solution being designed, and this enchantment is attributed to the perfect combination of form, functionality and usability.

When it came to visuals, the designer informant in the survey lamented the fact that the designer's work is often considered only in terms of how something looks, as the following unit shows: "(...) *So the designer's work is always thought of as visual only*" (L487- I5). This unit indicates the designer's need to be perceived not only for the subjective aesthetic part, which exists and is not denied, but also the request for recognition for the objective part of the activity, which involves methodology and decision-making techniques present in its processuality.

With regard to competence (c) - applying imagination and constructive forethought to practical problems, it was possible to see from the analysis of the information that it was reinforced by both designers and non-designers.

The ability to imagine and creativity were skills cited as essential by the informants for working as a designer, as shown in the following unit: "(...) *I think there's the creativity part, normally developers are very Cartesian, very square, and designers have this creative side. I think that if you're not creative, you can't do it. You have to be able to imagine the colors, understand the client and be able to reproduce a brand, a design, you have to have a lot of creativity.*" (L65-69 - I1 ).

This competence is directly related to the idea that shaping something requires creative and analytical skills, presented by Lowgren and Stolterman (1998), in this sense the authors are in agreement in the light of the information gathered in this research.

In the context investigated, the designer has direct contact with the client during the initial phase of the project. At this stage, the designer has the responsibility of constructing a briefing which contains information about the context and needs of the client and user. It is this information that will inform the creation of the solution. This contact with the client and the collection of information therefore implies the need for good communication skills in order to be able to extract the important information from the client and also to communicate a solution proposal to the client.

Rationality is required in order to make a choice that involves the best options for the context and the client. This choice involves considering different variables, both more and less important, and choosing the best path for the project based on reason. These statements are supported by the information gathered in this research.

It is this ability to analyze the information in a context and imaginatively create solutions based on this information that allows the designer to make ideas tangible, in other words, to transport an idea from the abstract to the visual and concrete.

This perception becomes even more evident when considering the context studied and the solutions generated by the designers investigated in this context, where the graphic interface of websites and systems for the internet are the most concrete thing within a virtual product, a website for the internet.

In order to carry out this task of shaping something, the designer in the context used is asked to use his analytical skills to understand the context of the client and user and the problem to be solved, so that he can detect the most important aspects, the most significant variables with which he can work on building a solution. Based on this analysis, the designer uses his or her creative skills to conceive a proposed solution, as was reported at various points in the research by designers and non-designers alike.

However, this ability is related to another, which is to understand that deciding requires critical thinking, as stated by Lowgren and Stolterman (1998) and also directly cited in the statements of the informants in this research, as shown in the following unit: "(...) *He has to have a critical sense to discuss the idea, have a good power of argument, he has to be creative...*" (L288- 289 - I2).

Although difficult to define, critical thinking can be understood as the ability to make an in-depth assessment of a situation or context in order to make an appropriate choice of solution to a problem. In the context studied, it can be seen that the service most exposed to criticism is that of the designer. Several times the informants mentioned critical thinking as a necessary skill for designers. The need for designers to learn how to deal with criticism, receive it, process it and accept it was also pointed out, and this is also related to their critical capacity.

This ability allows the best choice to be made between the options imagined and created by the designer, based on the context of the solution. This capacity will also allow the input of information from other members of the multidisciplinary teams in which the designer works, so that new ideas and values can be added to the solution to be developed, improving it.

Regarding the competence of (d) - use of non-verbal resources such as drawings/graphics/media/spatial modeling, among other means of communication, as a means of modeling problem solving, it can be said that this competence was cited directly and indirectly by the non-designer informants investigated as being specific to the designer. Some even considered it to be a natural gift, a skill that is born with the individual and that most professionals in the exact sciences do not possess, as the following units show: (...) it may not even be a sketch.) it *may not even be a sketch, but there's a drawing of a process, there's a sketch, an image, something visual, you know, that makes it easier to understand.* (L390-391 - I2) or in "(...) *he has more visual reasoning, more refined, he can give shape to ideas, which we have difficulty with...*" (L1504-1505 - I5).

This competence is related to Lowgren and Stolterman's (1998) definition, which states that the design of aesthetic properties requires the ability to shape and compose, which is reaffirmed by the research information. In order to give form, the designer seems to use a series of non-verbal resources to express himself and make his idea tangible.

In relation to designers, this notion was also present but was less emphasized, which may also be due to the notion that it is a basic, even obvious, skill for working as a designer. However, more important for designers is the power of synthesis, and visual reasoning itself is already a means of synthesizing abstract information and ideas, giving them form, which results in a graphic representation that can be a sketch, a drawing, a *wireframe*, a *layout,* in short a visual solution.

In this way, it is possible to verify the ability to make people see in the informants' perception of their imaginative, creative and visual reasoning ability to give shape to ideas through drawings, modeling, prototyping and various non-verbal resources. Thus, based on the information collected and constructed (see), and the permanent critical process of questioning the future, the designer's skills make it possible to make ideas tangible through the artifacts they create, even if these are part of virtual worlds such as the internet, as was the case with the company observed.

Still on the subject of the use of non-verbal resources and means of communication as a means of modeling solutions, it is a fact that this competence only becomes useful in relationships with other individuals, such as clients, users and even teammates, which is related to another capacity mentioned by de Lowgren and Stolterman (1998), when they state that working with clients requires rationality and communicative capacity. In this sense, the ability to communicate is of great importance as a skill to be mobilized by designers in their practical work, especially when taking into account the context of the teams and social groups in which they work. This statement finds support in units of analysis such as: "(...) *I think it's very important to exchange information, communication, that idea that it's not my job, it's our job. If we make a mistake, we make a mistake, it's not you who's wrong and that thing about everyone feeling responsible. If we're working on this project and we have this deadline, I'm not the one who has to demand it, everyone has to work together, this awareness. I think the team has to be a team...*" (L971-976 - I4) who explain the need for clear communication and information sharing when working in teams.

The unit above also serves to explain how transparency and sharing information is linked to a sense of collectivity, teamwork, or as the unit itself puts it, a team. More than just a consequence of good communication skills, transparency indicates the need for a standard of ethics, or the right way of doing things. Achieving this standard requires the mobilization of values and ideals on the part of team members and this is in line with what Lowgren and Stolterman (1998) said when they defined that ethical properties require a vision and knowledge of values and ideals.

Aesthetics, functionality and usability are issues that need to be mobilized by an ethical conduct of the process, where everyone realizes the importance of their activity and integration with other areas, and that this is done with recognition, respect and autonomy. In an environment of trust and a sense of responsibility.

It can be said, based on the analysis of the statements made by the designers and non-designers, that this ethics and knowledge of values and ideals should apply to everyone involved in the process of developing a solution.

Whether it's the client, who actively participates in this process and needs to be considered in their context, which involves their values and ideals, or within project teams, where these ethical skills are required in order to establish an environment of trust, of teamwork, a collective sense that amplifies the strength and potential of the team, and consequently of its members.

Regarding the ability to (e) - adopt strategies focusing on solutions, it can be said that during the information gathering/construction techniques of this research, it was possible to see that the designers' entire work process, which was observed and reported in the focus group and in-depth interviews, always focused on the solution to be generated for a problem or need of the client and users, and that often the definition of the problem and the solution occurred simultaneously.

Even though the process initially takes place through the designer gathering information and getting to know the context, it is implicit that this process only begins in order to build a solution for the client.

The visual reasoning skills mentioned above can reinforce the idea that the focus is always on developing a solution to a problem. Another important factor worth mentioning about the focus on the solution is that, in the context studied, although the designer participates in the project to build this solution from the outset, the real start of the company's relationship with the client takes place beforehand, in commercial spheres where the company offers a solution (website/system) to the client, or the client requests this solution from the company, i.e. it is already known in advance that the solution to be developed will be a website or internet system (software), so the information gathering strategy and the process of building the solution are focused on this.

Another important aspect worth discussing here is that, in fact, the solution resulting from a design process, within the company studied, cannot be considered the ideal, perfect or optimal solution, but rather a satisfactory solution that aims to solve a problem for the client and/or users, and which is always developed in parallel with several other solutions so that the best path is chosen. This definition goes hand in hand with another skill stated by Cross (1992), which is the ability to (f) employ abductive thinking and work with several alternative design solutions in parallel in order to understand the problem-solution space.

Abductive reasoning or thinking does not give the truth, but works with probabilities. The ability to work with different possibilities and probabilities in order to solve a problem has been widely affirmed by designers and non-designers alike as a desirable skill for a designer to have.

However, due to the number of demands and the short time to develop them, the common reality of the context investigated does not allow for a very large number or even several alternative solutions in parallel. What happens is that the designers investigated sometimes develop at most two proposals, so that the client is given a choice between one path or the other. In this sense, the options developed by the designer directly aid a better understanding of the problem and already constitute a graphic-visual proposal for a solution to this problem.

Another factor that generates the need for new and more complex skills is the advance of information and communication technology, which is increasingly providing new tools and new concepts, methods and techniques for contemporary designers, requiring them to constantly search for updates and new knowledge.

Designers therefore need to be permanently open-minded about learning. This need is perceived in units such as: "(...) *Technology helps design, as soon as you upgrade technology, design goes along with it, design sometimes forces technology to move.*" (L 1268-1269 - I7). Considering the context of an information technology company, such as the one observed in this research, this need to monitor technology and its design possibilities proved to be of fundamental importance to the designers and non-designers investigated.

This relationship with technology is in line with what was also mentioned by Lowgren and Stolterman (1998), when they stated that the design of structural properties requires discernment and knowledge of technology, which can be seen in the following unit: "(...) *It's no use wanting to design good things for people and not knowing anything about the support, the materials, the latest techniques...*" (L317- 318-I3).

Being involved in the design of a site/system from the outset, contributing heavily to determining the structure of the solutions and, even in the case of a virtual space, where the solution developed by the designer is located in the context investigated in this research, the design of a site/system for the Internet, in other words, software, necessarily implies that the designer develops knowledge about the support of his solution and the technologies involved. In some of the speeches, it was even possible to see that it is this up-to-date knowledge of the available technologies that will allow processes to be carried out that until recently were considered impossible, precisely because of the limitations of the technology.

When considering the context in which this research was carried out, a public organization (company), and more specifically in the social group of multidisciplinary teams, it became clear that there was a need to observe skills that were not only technical and related to methods, techniques, tools and technology. It was also necessary to focus on the designer's personality and the attributes of this personality that relate to relationships with other individuals, which will be discussed below.

Let's now analyze the words of Flaviano Celaschi:

> "The designer has become a key operator in the world of production and consumption, whose knowledge is typically multidisciplinary due to his way of reasoning about the product itself, because he is at the center of the relationship between consumption and production, due to the need to understand the preferences and dynamics of the value network and, above all, because his actions must be able to modify or confer new values on products through his design interventions." (CELASCHI, 2000).

In the context studied and during the techniques used to collect and construct information, it was possible to identify the perception of non-designers about the designer's role as mediator in the statements made by the informants, as the following unit points out: "(...) *Intermediator I think, I think that would be the best word, intermediator. Between the data and the information, between the source and the destination, you know? He would be in the middle "..." in that middle ground.*" (L544-546 - I3). This role seemed much more important to non-designers than to the designers themselves, who admitted this competence in a more indirect way.

To play this multidisciplinary role, specific and interrelated skills are required, such as the ability to connect different areas of knowledge, the ability to understand different languages and even develop new ones, and the ability to be an interpreter, as the following unit shows: "(...) *And also to be that person who suddenly manages to give that idea not only in the work, manages to complement the team in a multidisciplinary way, to connect and communicate with different areas, I think that in this part of web projects especially this is fundamental and this is what the designer does.*" (L894-898 - I4), a statement that is in line with what Celaschi (2000) said.

In the context studied, the designer's work is actually between production and consumption in the sense that he works for a company that develops websites and systems for the internet, and in these contexts he is responsible for the interfaces between two things, in this case between complex computer systems (software) and citizens.

Working in this context, the designer needs to be attentive to issues of usability and ergonomics, in order to adapt these systems and sites to human conditions by modifying them, always making it easier for users to use them and carry out their tasks. This requires the power of observation, information filtering, the power of synthesis, permanent research, trial and error and a permanent willingness to learn new methods, techniques and technologies. Only by mobilizing all these skills will the designer be able to achieve the goal of satisfying a user's desire or need. These skills were mentioned by both designers and non-designers during the course of the research, as can be seen in the following unit: "(...) *And also being that person who suddenly manages to give that idea not only in the work, manages to complement the team in a multidisciplinary way, to connect and communicate with different areas, I think that in this part of web projects especially, this is fundamental and this is what the designer does.*" (L894-898 - I4).

Complementing the previous ideas, it is important to consider the concepts of design management, which define design as an activity that plays a primarily instrumental role in business processes. The author presents design as an activity that has four levels of influence on the organization: as a differentiator, as an integrator, as a transformer and as good business for society, (MOZOTA, 2003).

Given the information collected and the organization observed, it was possible to perceive these influences on the designer's work. At various points in the speech of designers and non-designers, the expectation of the different, the unusual, the surprising was noted in relation to the designer's work. This expectation is materialized in an essential attribute of the designer, who, due to his different profile from the majority of the company's professionals, and his close relationship with art perceived by these same professionals, has the almost exclusive responsibility of enchanting the client and/or user through the creation of the new, which indicates the perception of a close relationship between his activity and innovation.

In this sense, working in teams, serving different clients and seeking to understand different contexts, the designer at the company investigated regularly integrates knowledge, people and objectives in order to transform realities through their work, as the following unit points out: "(...) *Because the designer has several, shall we say, applications. But within software development, in our context here at PROCERGS, I see the designer as an important part when we need several fronts, to connect different areas...*" (L20-22 - I1).

With regard to the last aspect presented by Mozota (2003), in the case of a public company where the designer works developing interfaces between systems and citizens, it was clear to both designers and non-designers that all the work the designer is involved in has a greater purpose, which is to serve the citizen, to make their tasks and lives easier.

In the selected units of analysis, it can be seen that the solutions developed by designers are good business for society, since their remit and their work are always aimed at serving it in the best possible way, as the following unit shows: "(...) *The designer is the guy who says, I don't just need this, I have to have a screen that tells me how the car behind me is doing, how the car in front of me is doing, I have to have a seat that hugs me better, I have to improve, make people's lives easier, I have to try to interpret and improve every aspect to make things better and better, more suited to what users need.* " (L1518-1522 - I5), where the search for continuous improvement of solutions, the search to do things differently and in a way that suits the user's needs is seen as the responsibility of designers.

With regard to the set of competencies proposed by Nigel Cross (1992) and Lowgren and Stolterman (1998), it was clear from this research that, although these studies were carried out more than 20 years ago, many of their concepts are still valid in today's contexts in which designers work, as is the case with the company studied.

However, it is also clear that this set of competencies is still not enough to bring together all the skills a designer needs to work in teams. This set of skills needs to be better specified, detailed and deepened. In addition, given the social group and organizational context of the multidisciplinary teams investigated, where the designer works, these aspects add new needs regarding competences to the design process and, consequently, to the designer, especially with regard to relationships and integrated action with other individuals.

Therefore, in addition to discussing the competence profiles presented by Cross (1992) and Lowgren and Stolterman (1998), it is necessary to go further and discuss the concept of social competence presented by Asendorpf (2004) and complemented by Thorndike (1920).

According to Asendorpf (2004):

> the concept of social competence includes two distinct groups of skills:
>
> • The ability to impose oneself in social situations, i.e. the ability to defend one's own interests
>
> • The ability to build relationships, i.e. the ability to initiate positive relationships and maintain them. (ASENDORPF, 2004)

In other words, in order to work in teams and relate to other individuals, people need to be able to defend their interests without forgetting that they are relating to other people. Thorndike (1920) calls these two aspects of social competence social sensitivity - the ability to put oneself in someone else's shoes - and social action skills - the ability to deal with difficult social situations (THORNDIKE, 1920).

When we look at designers working in collective contexts, as was the case in this research, we see that, in addition to the competences mentioned above and almost all confirmed by the study carried out, other competences are mobilized, especially with regard to relationship competences with other individuals, as the following unit shows: "(...) *The designer has to take part in the initial meetings with the business analyst, understand the problem with the client, talk to the systems team, with the analyst, he always has to be with the team.*" (L 291-297 - I3), highlighting the designer's need for participation and presence, which also requires interpersonal communication between colleagues and with the client.

Others referred directly to the need for emotional balance in order to be able to manage the conflicts and tensions that arise in team interaction, as the following unit shows: "(...) *Until recently we saw that designers, for the most part, didn't know how to manage tensions. As they say in medicine, emeraldite syndrome, everyone wanting to be the best, to be a star and to beat each other up and so on...*" (L821-824-I7) quoted by a designer, which indicates a self-awareness of the need to be prepared for these design situations. It is important to note here that for both designers and non-designers, and because they work in teams, the need to know how to deal with conflicts and tensions that arise in these interactions with others was evident. Therefore, skills such as flexibility, open-mindedness, acceptance of criticism, character, honesty and trust were clearly perceived in the statements made by the informants as being important skills in building relationships and in gaining a deeper understanding of the contexts and situations of both the clients and the team.

For non-designers, on the other hand, other relationship attributes were more often cited, such as flexibility, the ability to accept criticism and feedback from users and colleagues, a sense of collectivity and communication, seen here with more emphasis on the ability to listen and share information than to express it verbally or non-verbally, as indicated by the following unit: "(...) *Willing to share what you know and receive criticism or suggestions, without seeing it as negative criticism, I think that's teamwork... you think about the success of the whole, not the individual. There's no point in me doing my bit if the others can't do theirs, we've lost the game, there's no point in me doing my bit.*" (L137-141-I1).

In view of what was observed in the statements made by the informants, it became clear that these skills are extremely important when the context in which they work is multidisciplinary teams, made up of different people from different areas of knowledge. In this sense, various relationship skills necessary for the good performance of the team and its members were mentioned, which designers should possess in order to work in these contexts.

Empathy or the ability to put oneself in the other person's shoes, whether that other person is the client, the user or the members of the team, was frequently cited as an important attribute of designers. This attribute enables them to better understand contexts, situations, people and relationships, as can be seen in the following unit: "(...) *You have to see the role of the user, the client and the developer, right. You have to put yourself in their shoes.*" (L283-284-I2).

The study in question allowed us to see that it is not enough for a designer to possess a set of technical skills in order to act as such. In the organizations of contemporary society, such as the company studied, and in teams, the designer, in order to serve clients, necessarily needs to relate, and in this sense another set of skills can be listed as important for the smooth running of the design activity. These involve communication skills, character, ethics and personality that go beyond the typical technical knowledge of design.

5.2 ON HUMAN-CENTERED DESIGN, USER-CENTERED DESIGN AND INTERACTION DESIGN

The importance given to the user was evident during the content analysis of the statements made by designers and non-designers. Due to the nature of the solution that the designer designs in multidisciplinary teams, in the case of the company observed, websites and public service systems for the Internet, it is clear that the user is always at the center of attention in the design process.

However, it became clear that even in a multidisciplinary team and in the case of a complex solution made up of different skills, the concern for the user and the human aspects involved in the interaction is the responsibility of the designer. This can be seen *in* the following units: *"(...) He's the guy who designs to graphically communicate something, some need, who is concerned with the appearance, the shape of the product and how it should look to delight its user."* (L1061-1062-I6). In this case, the informant used a combination of skills involving communication, graphic expression and relating this to the shape and appearance of the product with the ultimate aim of enchanting the user of the solution. The responsibility taken on by the designer for the interface between man and computer can be clearly seen in the following unit: *"(...) The role of the designer here and as I see it would be the graphic interface, the visual and graphic art part, conceptualizing for the whole issue of websites that we develop and systems."* (L2360-2362-I7).

This concern seems to have become evident due to the fact that the company analyzed is an information technology company and the fact that the designer develops his activity with the aim of designing websites and service systems on the Internet. In these contexts, functionality and ease of use of the solutions is constantly sought through the application of ergonomics and usability concepts. This ease of use can be seen in the following unit: *"(...) Thinking about PROCERGS and the government, the best thing for us, as designers here, would be for someone to say something like, "Gee, I had to pay my fine there. Man, that's easy. I took my cell phone here, gave it three taps, received it at home... that would be the pinnacle."* (L1026-1029-I3), where the designer realizes the importance of simplifying the tasks that would be carried out through an online service accessed through an interface, which would be his responsibility.

This facilitation of task execution requires the designer to observe the human aspects involved in the interaction, as well as the use of the solution they develop in order to improve this interaction, which is in line with what (NORMAN, 2006), (SHARP, ROGERS and PREECE, 2002), (WINOGRAD, 1997) said in the theoretical framework of this research.

This attribution is also perceived by non-designers, who affirm the importance of the designer, as the following unit shows: "(...) *So I think he fits into one of the important roles, very important for software development, to achieve the goal, which is the satisfaction of the client and the user.*" (L35-36-I1) or in "(...) *And there's also this very technical part of not getting too heavy, I think you have to know a lot about system development, and the user, right, how they think about navigating, the layout of the navigation, you have to know it well to help set up the interfaces.*" (L70-72-I1), which shows that the development of interfaces must take into account the human and user aspects of the solution in order to be able to design increasingly optimized, simpler and more satisfactory interactions for clients and users.

5.3 DIFFICULTIES FACED BY DESIGNERS IN CARRYING OUT THEIR WORK

In order to gain a deeper understanding of the role and skills of a designer working in multidisciplinary teams, this research considered the difficulties faced by designers working in these contexts. These difficulties were frequent in the statements made by the designers and required them to be classified into subcategories of analysis so that they could be observed with greater focus.

Thus, the subcategories relating to the difficulties faced by designers were the conceptualization of design and the designer, the definition of objectivity and subjectivity and the relationship with art, communication and access to information, autonomy at work, training, educational, academic, curricular, the lack of regulation of the profession, respect and professional recognition and the difficulties of the organization studied.

With regard to the conceptualization of the activity, the professional and the terms that refer to them, design and designer, what we noticed is that there is a lot of confusion about this on the part of non-designers and there is a perception that this difficulty in definition has the implication of a lack of recognition, respect and appreciation of the full potential of the designer. In units such as: "(...) *and then who will respect you when you say you're a designer? Then, if they ask you what you are, you can't even answer properly.*" (L529-530-I5) this is quite clear.

The difficult definition of the activity, already mentioned when talking about the historical evolution of the definitions presented by ICSID, and perceived in the speeches of the designers themselves who took part in the focus group, has the consequence of making non-designers more uncomfortable, who, without knowing exactly what design is about, end up distancing themselves or simply not respecting it or considering it important. One factor that complicates this perception, especially in a Portuguese-speaking country like Brazil, is the use of English terms to define it, which, while on the one hand can add an aspect of sophistication to the activity, on the other hand makes it even more difficult to understand, given the difficult translation of the term, which can mean completely different activities in Portuguese, such as project and drawing.

However, the very use of these two possible terms to translate the term design from English into Portuguese already reveals some of the essential aspects that characterize this activity, since the skills of drawing and visual reasoning, combined with the planning of actions through a project process, were frequently mentioned in the statements of the informants as skills necessary for good design performance.

When the difficulties reported referred to the definition of the objectivity and subjectivity of the activity and its relationship with art, it became clear from the research that the perception on the part of designers is that this lack of clarity in the definition makes non-designers perceive the designer only in terms of behavioral and creative aspects, as if they were artists, people who are different in the way they think and act. In this way, they end up building a distorted image of the activity, which emphasizes the subjective aspects much more, sometimes even disregarding the objective part.

According to Cardoso (CARDOSO, 2013) the characteristics would be:

> (a) systemic thinking, understood as the ability to understand complex systems considering the elements and relationships between them; (b) inventiveness of language, which would be the ability to create, understand, manipulate and combine different languages, which are generally visual in nature and (c) craftsmanship, which can be understood as a high degree of attention to detail and care in the execution of the task, stemming from a peculiar sense of pride in the work, the pleasure of doing it well. It is worth discussing attributes (b) inventiveness of language and (c) craftsmanship as they relate to art and design (CARDOSO, 2013).

As well as considering the system in his way of thinking, the designer needs to integrate knowledge to combine these elements, he needs to understand different languages, different audiences and different needs. In order to achieve these objectives, they need to be open to learning, understanding and even creating languages that facilitate communication and understanding between the elements of the system they are part of.

This requires a deep understanding of languages, a search for the different and the unexpected, as well as knowledge of the technologies involved and available, so that they can act as interpreters in the multidisciplinary contexts in which they work. These characteristics require them to behave in a truly different way, seeking to construct meanings based on a work process, a process of generating knowledge and learning and, consequently, of discovering the unknown, like science, religion and very closely related to art (which also involves methods and techniques).

With regard to *craftsmanship, it's worth* noting that the statements made by the informants in this study made it clear that skills such as good taste, attention to detail and rigor are important for working as a designer. These skills are related to *craftsmanship,* as the following unit shows: "(...) *The designer... in 99% of cases, he has good taste, so that's a great skill that a person needs to have to work as a designer: good taste, good references and experience...*" (L1500-1503 - I5).

It is clear from this study that the relationship between design and art is much broader. In this relationship, various attributes of art are found in the design activity, which can sometimes be perceived negatively or positively. However, it would be an exaggeration to say that design is all about art and to dismiss all the wealth of objective and technical knowledge in the profession. It is more accurate to understand design as a hybrid activity, which uses subjective and objective aspects to conceive original solutions adapted to the reality of its users.

When the difficulty reported referred to a lack of communication, units such as: "(...) *It's even a question of, I'm going to make a beautiful, wonderful layout, but I can't find the information...*" were noticed. (L 503-504 - I6), that access to the information needed to properly understand the problem and generate the solution is often not available, which refers to the designer's already discussed ability to tolerate the lack of ill-defined or non-existent information (CROSS, 1994) and also confirms what was presented by Lowgren and Stolterman (1998), when they affirmed the need for good communication skills to work as a designer.

Following on from the discussion of the difficulties encountered by the designer, there were speeches with references to autonomy at work, understood here as control over one's own professional performance, and it was possible to see this in units such as: "(...) *Yes, there are problems in the execution part too, that you (designer) do one way and then it's not as you designed it because someone decided to tamper with your work...*" (L 519-521 - I2) that there are interferences during the designer's work and even in the finished work.

This perceived lack of autonomy is directly related to a lack of professional respect and recognition of the importance of the activity. Therefore, the designer needs to establish methods, techniques and devices so that he can guarantee that his part of the work will not be interfered with by other professionals.

One consequence of this is that the designers at the company under investigation are increasingly getting involved with tasks that are not within their remit, such as code programming, since their knowledge of this activity gives them greater control over the appearance, functionality and usability of the solution they design.

In some moments of the designers' speeches, it was also possible to perceive a certain difficulty in terms of the educational, academic and curricular training of the designer, in the sense that they pointed to the design teaching institutions as being partly responsible for the inadequate training of the designer to act as such, as the following units show: "(...) *The faculty is not prepared to train you as a professional, really...*" (L 538-539 - I5) or in "(...) *the market needs a professional and then colleges rush to fill this space.*" (L 555-556 - I6).

The designers also referred to a specific situation of the design profession in Brazil, which is the lack of regulation of the profession. This aspect results in a greater lack of recognition for the activity and its practitioners, as the following units show: "(...) *One problem is the fact that we are not regulated...*" (L542-I2) or in "(...) *It's another very specific situation. Our profession isn't even regulated.*" (L 544 - I5). It is therefore possible to see from the designers' statements that they consider that regulating the design activity could strengthen the activity in the sense of standardizing both the training for working as such and other specific issues in the activity such as salaries and career levels, as well as defining the profession more clearly, reducing ambiguities through regulation, which should begin with a clearer definition of the profession.

It is important to note here that at the beginning of the research there was already a bill for regulation in the national congress, but until the beginning of 2015 it had not been sanctioned by the President of the Republic to be valid throughout the country.

Finally, it is important to discuss the difficulties specific to the organization studied, which were frequently mentioned by both designer and non-designer informants and which directly influence the designer's role in the context observed. It was common to find statements such as: "(...) *I think that basically all the problems come from that history, every 4 years everything changes.*" (L691-692-I1). This unit makes clear the difficulty caused by the management changes that take place in the company every four years, given that the company is public and administered by managers appointed politically by the state governor.

Another important aspect to consider is that previous work to raise awareness and introduce design and integrate the designer with other professionals has already been carried out with good results, but the periodic changes in the company's management mean that sometimes the work of raising awareness and clarifying the activity of design is lost or ignored due to these changes in management.

Also related to the specific difficulties of the company observed is the fact that the professionals are hired via public tender, and even though their work regime is governed by the CLT (Consolidation of Labor Laws), the company's employees are granted stability, which means that people join the company and are unlikely to leave. As a result, many even officially retire but continue to work for the company in order to maintain their financial conditions.

As a result, there is a clash of generations within the company, which has professionals hired on different competitions and belonging to different generations, from new recruits to employees who have been with the company since it was founded (over 40 years). This makes it difficult to standardize concepts and knowledge within the company, which directly influences the role of the designer in the organization, as the following unit points out: *"(...) People, I think the IT company with the highest average age in the world. There are people who left a brick factory and came here and still make bricks, you know? They've never updated."* (L1527-1529-I7). This difficulty is also related to the influence of organizational culture on the role of the designer, which will be discussed below to conclude the tens about the difficulties faced by the designer.

Understood as the set of formal and informal rules and agreements, habits, methods and techniques that a company acquires over time, the organizational culture was mentioned several times by the informants as a factor of great influence on the designer's work, acting as a brake and restricting the use of the designer's full potential, as the following units show: *"(...) Then comes the question of organizational culture, right? Ah, it's always been like this, it's how we work..."* (L1562-1563-I4) or in *"(...) I think the company culture does have a bit of an influence, not least because we have those ways of working, standards, methods, rules and even hierarchy, right, and all this puts a bit of a brake on the designer. "* (L1049-1051 - I4).

There is a clear perception among designers and non-designers that the organizational culture inevitably influences the work of designers, restricting them. This implies that designers need to adapt and develop ways of overcoming this difficulty by getting to know the strengths and weaknesses of this culture, so that they can gradually show the real possibilities of their activity. This can be achieved, for example, by constantly raising awareness and presenting design so that all sectors of the company are aware of its existence and the activities and competencies that are its responsibility. Since this is an information technology company, with a focus on computer and communication services, it is gradually becoming aware of the need for the designer's knowledge and how this professional can add value to the integrated solutions it develops.

## 5.4 THE DESIGNER'S MULTIPLE ROLES

The aim of this research was to reflect on the role and competencies of the designer in multidisciplinary teams. However, after analyzing the information gathered, we realized that the role of the designer is not just one, but several within a team. A multiple role, which adapts to the contexts in which it operates, the organization, the team and the individuals, whether they are clients or teammates.

With regard to these multiple roles, it is important to present what is considered to be a list of the most important roles detected in this research.

On several occasions, both designer and non-designer informants pointed to the role of mediator as being the designer's own. Whether between clients and users, between the market and the company under investigation, or between machines and their systems, information and people.

In many passages of the content analyzed, the perception of the designer's position in the middle, between two different areas, was evident. This indicates another competence that would be mobilized in this task, which is the ability to interpret and translate and to connect different areas and knowledge. This becomes clear in passages such as: "(...) *Intermediator I think, I think that would be the best word, intermediator. Between the data and the information, between the source and the destination, you know? He would be in the middle, in that middle ground.*" (L544-546-I3) present in the statements of non-designers, who emphasized the importance of this role.

This other role of interpreter of contexts, situations and people was also frequently mentioned and reinforced during the research techniques, as the following unit shows "(...) *He's an interpreter, he's in the middle helping to translate needs, he's a mediator.*" (L1488-1489-I5). Units like this indicate the designer's own perception of the ability to deal with different languages, different audiences and needs, and that it would be the professional's job, for example, to initially understand the ill-defined context of the client and the solution to be developed and then translate this to the project team through their vision, which is in line with what Cross (1994) said.

This role can be seen as an outgrowth of the mediator's role discussed earlier, since those who position themselves as intermediaries between two different realities will probably only be able to make a connection between these two parties if they can understand the languages and objectives involved, and reconcile them by communicating one side with the other.

Part of the resources the designer uses to act as a mediator and interpreter come from the specific technical knowledge of the area, which also gives them the role of technician, as is clear from passages such as: "(...) There's *no point in wanting to design good things for people and not knowing anything about the support, the materials, the latest techniques...*" (L317-318-I3). In this way, competences relating to information architecture, specific methods and techniques, knowledge of colors, layout, composition, ergonomics, usability and functionality of solutions and technology were recalled at various points in the speeches.

Finally, with regard to the designer's multiple roles in multidisciplinary teams, it is important to emphasize the role of artist, which became evident during the research and, even though there was disagreement between designers and non-designers about the effects of this relationship on the designer's professional recognition, the fact is that this role exists, and in the context investigated, this role is the total responsibility of the designer who is the type of professional who stands out from the others, mostly professionals from exact areas such as systems analysts, business analysts, programmers and administrators (managers).

The relationship between design activity and art was perceived in this research in completely different ways by the designers and non-designers investigated. When this relationship came up in the designers' speeches, it was always in the sense that this relationship harms the designer's image and work, because it adds to the work of the designer.

subjective attributes of art to an activity considered by the designers themselves to be much more objective than subjective.

It was clear to the designers that their professional activity is based on methods, rules and techniques, so that the choices made during the design process are the result of study and research and not the result of artistic inspiration. This is in line with what Cardoso (2013) says when he states that:

> From the 20th century onwards, some schools of design scholars began to consider design an activity based on scientific concepts, disregarding its relationship with art (Cardoso, 2013).

This is also reflected in the behavior of the designers investigated. Whenever they referred to this relationship with art, the designers showed discontent and disagreement, believing that this relationship undermines the seriousness of their work and, consequently, respect and professional recognition within the context investigated, as exemplified by the following unit: "(...) *Art is totally subjective and design not always...*" (L474 - I2).

As well as not putting the responsibility for their work down to inspiration or choices made based on subjective criteria, another factor that caused the designers discontent when they looked at the relationship with art was the behavioral aspect, as the following unit shows: "(...) *Mainly because of this confusion, I think it messes with the arts, I think the guy is an artist, someone with difficult behavior.*" (L1144-1145-I4). A common perception in the content analysis was that this relationship attributes to designers behavioral traits typical of artists, which leads to a preconception of designers.

In this sense, expressions such as: difficult temperament, the delicate, the complicated, the alternative people, who travel, who see things in a different and unusual way were attributed to the designer because he possessed this artistic character in his activity. This analogy has often led to a distorted and pre-conceived view of the designer, as if he were considered an artist, with all his virtues and defects. Although this behavioral aspect was perceived by both designers and non-designers, it was the only point of agreement between the two audiences investigated regarding their relationship with art.

The non-designers, on the other hand, considered this relationship, several times during the interviews, to be perhaps the greatest difference in the designers' approach to the problems that arise in their work, in the teams and in the company investigated. This differential is characterized precisely by the ability to see situations from other angles not perceived by professionals from more rigid or exact areas, such as the vast majority of the company studied. In this sense, designers are perceived by non-designers as the most sensitive people, an ability that enables them to interpret the contexts and problems of clients and users more correctly.

Sometimes, this relationship with art has also been seen as a special gift, a natural tendency that is born with the individual, like a talent that only certain profiles of people possess and that system analysts, programmers and business analysts don't have, which in a way reinforces the value that non-designers place on the designer's relationship with art.

The most obvious thing is that, in a way, both sides are right in their arguments. The fact is that the designer can't just be considered an artist and thus completely ignore all the objective knowledge that he needs to develop in order to design solutions, and on which he bases his choices at the moment of creation, nor just a cold and calculating technician who bases all his choices on objective and exact criteria.

It is therefore necessary for non-designers to perceive the objective side of the activity more clearly, so as to recognize that the resulting choices presented by a designer in a website layout or system, such as colors, shapes and diagramming, for example, have been made on the basis of researched and established studies and knowledge, and not on the basis of random artistic inspiration. And the designer himself also needs to admit that his closeness to art is what allows him to design original and unexpected solutions that delight clients and users, which allows complex issues to be resolved through solutions that consider aesthetics, form, beauty as well as functionality and usability.

In this way, those who define the designer as an artist simply attribute all the virtues and defects of the artist to the designer, and those who try to define the designer as a technician, who bases all his decisions on objective knowledge far removed from art, are mistaken. To conclude the discussion on the relationship between design and art, what cannot be denied is the fact that this relationship exists and is older and broader than what this research has been able to investigate, leaving this indication for future studies.

The fact is that, based on the findings of these multiple roles of the designer, the theme of this research can be put in the plural, updating it as a result of the information found for: the roles and competencies of the designer in multidisciplinary teams.

Based on the content analysis carried out for this research, it was possible to construct a profile of what would be considered the ideal set of skills and competencies that a designer should possess. We will now present the two ideal profiles that will serve to meet the specific objective of this research, which is to draw a parallel between the views of designers and non-designers on the role and competencies of the designer. In this way, the comparative table between the two visions is presented:

Table 5 - Comparative table of designer competencies

| DESIGNERS | NO DESIGNERS |
|---|---|
| **Technical skills** | **Technical skills** |
| • Design | • Systems |
| • Troubleshooting | • Ergonomics and Users |
| • Color theory | • Methods and techniques |
| • Composition | • Tools |
| • Layout | • Technology |
| • Information Architecture | • Communications (technical aspects) |

| | |
|---|---|
| • Ergonomics<br>• Usability<br>• Technology<br>• Supports and Materials<br>• Systems<br>• Communication (aspects technicians)<br>• Planning<br>• Research<br>**Non-technical skills**<br>**Non-Technical Individuals**<br>• Creativity<br>• Synthesis capacity<br>• Aesthetic sense<br>• Good taste<br>• Flexibility for new ideas<br>• Perspicacity<br>• Modesty | **Non-technical skills**<br>**Individual Non-Technical**<br>• Creativity<br>• Good taste<br>• Experience<br>• Openness to the new<br>• Adapting to change<br>• Critical sense<br>• Synthesis capacity<br>• Filtering information<br>• Honesty<br>• Proactivity<br>• Resilience<br>• Flexibility / Open-mindedness<br>• Detachment<br>• Visual reasoning<br>• Organization |
| • Humility<br>• Detachment<br>• Patience<br>• Intuition<br>• Simplicity<br>• Willingness to learn<br>• Focus<br>• Autonomy<br>**No Social Techniques**<br>• Tolerance<br>• Sense of collectivity and team<br>• Conflict management tensions<br>• Emotional Control<br>• Acceptance of criticism<br>• Interpersonal Communication<br>• Interaction | • Simplicity<br>• Interpretation<br>• Update<br>• A love of art and culture in general<br>**Social techniques**<br>• Empathy<br>• Involvement<br>• Communication (arguing and sharing information)<br>• Information sharing provisions<br>• Availability<br>• Acceptance of criticism and suggestions<br>• Conflict management and tensions<br>• Connection capacity |

Below is a summary figure of the two views on designer competences investigated (designers and non-designers), resulting from the sum of technical, non-technical and social competences mentioned in the information gathering/construction techniques. The division into colors was made to indicate the competencies mentioned by designers (in blue), non-designers (in green) and by both in red.

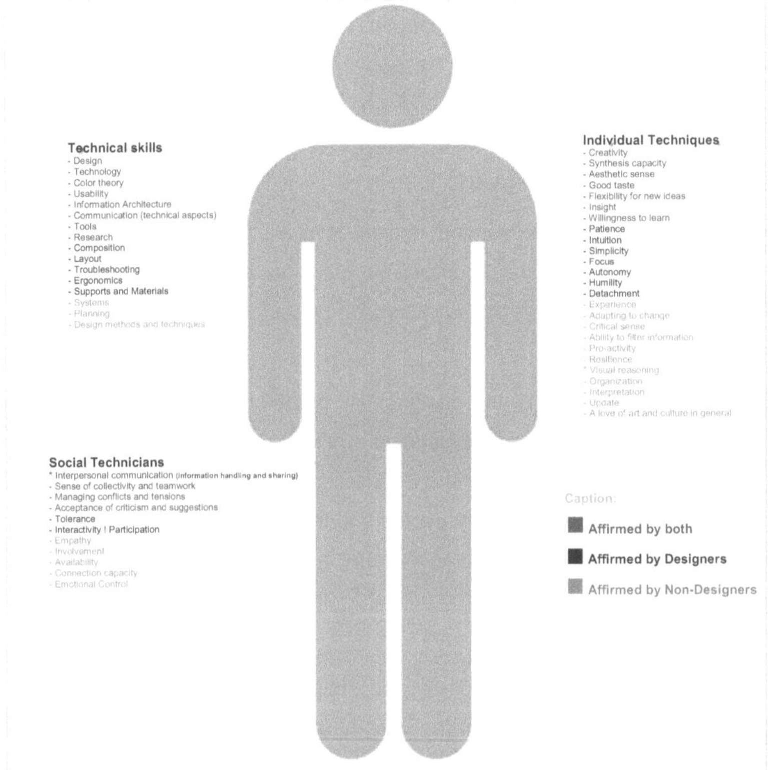


Figure 3 above helps us to understand that the understanding of the skills that a designer needs to have in order to work in the context observed is based on a consensus between the two views (designers and non-designers) most of the time. However, the differences between the views help to form a more complete picture of the competences to be mobilized by a designer, since they are complementary competences.

Studies that present this type of observation and synthesis can be especially useful for design education institutions that are interested in keeping up with the market and training design professionals who are prepared for the challenges of a complex and interconnected society.

# 6.  FINAL CONSIDERATIONS

With regard to the research objectives, it is believed that they were achieved, given that this research made it possible to identify the perceptions of designers and non-designers in the company under investigation about the role and competencies of the designer working in multidisciplinary teams. The result of combining these two perceptions was necessary in order to achieve a more complete and closer-to-reality view of what this role might be, and the skills required to perform it.

The research also made it possible to see that designers face a variety of difficulties when carrying out their work, and that these difficulties result in this role changing within companies, a dynamic of modification that is influenced by various aspects relating to the organizational context and culture.

This dynamic means that the role of the designer is sometimes perceived as static or restricted, sometimes expanding and sometimes shrinking, but certainly constantly changing. This dynamic requires designers and non-designers working in teams to be flexible and adaptable, whether in relation to people and their individual personalities, or in relation to the objectives of the organization as a whole, in short, in relation to the contexts and situations in which they work, so that the learning window can remain open, allowing for innovation, whether incremental or radical.

Among the strongest factors influencing this dynamic, this research also sought to reflect on the organizational culture of contemporary companies and its influence on the designer's work. What emerged, however, was that this culture, which sometimes seems to limit the organization's capacity for learning due to its rigidity, can be seen in another way, as the limiting walls of a path along which the designer must mobilize his role and skills in search of innovation and the satisfaction and facilitation of people's lives.

To do this, he will sometimes have to follow the rules, agreements, hierarchies and political guidelines of the organization, which may limit his full performance, but he can also sometimes use these same elements to rethink the relationships between them, and through research, exploration and creativity propose original and innovative solutions. In order to do this, they must always be aware of and adapt to change, an inherent aspect of contemporary society.

It also became clear that a company/organization needs to have the critical sense to understand that the only way to innovate is through learning, and learning requires flexibility, it requires people with different visions and knowledge living together and applying their knowledge to build complex solutions that meet the demands of today's society.

In view of the above, it is possible to state that, even though this is exploratory research, carried out through a case study, what determines its scientific limitations is that the information collected and built up together with the informants allows for a huge margin of interpretation given the large volume of information generated by the research techniques chosen, that the information collected and built up together with the informants allows for a huge range of interpretations given the large volume of information generated by the research techniques chosen (focus groups and interviews) and that these interpretations can be used as a basis for understanding this role and professional activity in greater depth.

The amount of information gathered and the number of interpretations generated by the research help to explain the extent and importance of the topic chosen. However, it is clear that in order to understand the role of the designer and the skills needed to perform it in a more in-depth and permanent way, it is necessary to observe more, to do more research into all the contexts in which the contemporary designer operates and not just organizations or companies. In today's world, designers are called upon to work in the most varied contexts, but what has become clear is that they no longer do anything on their own. They are in a system, part of a system as an influencing and influenced agent. This is why relationship or social skills are becoming increasingly important.

In this way, and meeting the specific objectives of this research, a reasonable reflection has been reached on the role and skills of the designer working in multidisciplinary teams, the general objective of this study. This reflection is already having practical effects on the organization studied, starting with a rethink of this role and skills and changes to work routines.

The definition of the method seemed to have been appropriate in terms of research techniques and the collection and construction of information, given that there were two audiences with views that contained similarities and differences on the subject, precisely what was explored in this research. Therefore, the choice of a focus group so that, for the first time in the company's history, most of the designers could be brought together to discuss their own role and competencies generated a relaxed and interested conversation where all the designers talked to each other as equals and this atmosphere of trust allowed significant information to be revealed during the technique.

With regard to non-designers, the approach required the use of a different information gathering/construction technique, precisely because it involved another type of professional stating their view of the designer, their role and competencies. In this case, it was more important to understand the image that non-designers had of the professional who works and integrates with them in the teams of the company studied.

With this focus on image, the semi-structured in-depth interview proved to be suitable, as it kept the focus of the interview and the questions on the subject and the research objectives and allowed the script to be directed more towards questions relating to the image that the non-designer had of the designer. It was also useful and efficient, as it brought the researcher closer to the informants and made it easier to apply in terms of the time available to carry out the research.

Still in relation to the method used in this research, it is important to note that the technique of content analysis proved to be suitable for a qualitative study of this type. This suitability was due, for example, to the need to create categories of competences, given that when reading the transcripts it was already possible to see that the competences naturally differed in terms of their nature, sometimes showing themselves to be technical, rather than individual and social (relationship) techniques. This categorization helped to organize the competence profiles perceived by designers and non-designers.

At the end of the content analysis, it was already possible to see that the visions contained significant similarities and differences that could be explored further. These similarities and differences also pointed to an ideal profile of competencies for working as a designer that was the result of both perceptions. In this way, a parallel was established between the two visions, one of the specific objectives of this research and which remains as one of the contributions of this research on a subject as broad and complex as the roles and competences for working as a designer, an area that is situated in the middle and as a connection between so many different areas of knowledge such as design.

The profile of competencies raised in this research between designers and non-designers, in their similarities and differences, represents an interesting contribution of this research, which can be especially useful when looking at what competencies and skills should be taught to professionals who intend to become designers in undergraduate courses, for example. This application of the results of this study could be especially useful for educational institutions, for example, which are trying to update their curricula to meet the needs of the market and of today's professionals.

Although the sentence above may seem obvious, people don't always have a clear understanding of a role and what skills are needed to play it. This research has shown that, in addition to possessing technical skills and competences, in order to act and be recognized, designers are involved in social processes that require other characteristics, requirements and skills, so that in the end they have a team that functions as such, that is, that thinks and acts collectively and collaboratively with a common goal, leveraging the strength of all its members.

Working with different professionals from different fields of knowledge, with different methods and references, and establishing formal and informal rules and agreements for the team's work, design is also a social process involving individuals and different interests. These relationships are influenced by diverse circumstances that the designer needs to know how to deal with and adapt to. This multidisciplinarity, characteristic of his field, then becomes his great differential as a professional, where he puts into practice his essential ability to connect different skills in order to meet the increasingly complex demands of contemporary society. Even more so if they are working in an organization or company that is naturally multidisciplinary, as was the case with the company we observed.

The opportunity to develop this research topic in the organization also represented a rare opportunity for non-designers, but especially for the company's designers, to discuss such a peculiar function within the company studied. This importance was perceived by all the participants.

In the focus group with designers, which lasted an hour and fifty minutes, this opportunity was so well received that the focus group technique practically had to be interrupted by the mediator, as the questions in the script had already been exhausted and the informants wanted to continue the discussion.

It is also important to note here that this discussion has led to a review and reformulation of the role of the designer and their official duties within the company under investigation. This process is ongoing and seeks to redefine the tasks and projects in which the designer is entitled to participate in the company, and the tasks that the designer is able to handle, as well as those that are not their responsibility. It is hoped that with the conclusion of this research, the results can be used in the company's practice, clarifying for the staff the real possibilities offered by working with a designer integrated into the teams.

The application of these results could also suggest ways and means of broadening the designer's role and importance within the company by presenting their profile and a list of services and skills to other professionals and sectors of the company.

In the context observed, the designer needs to understand that the solution they develop, in the case of this research, government websites and systems based on the Internet, are part of broader government policies and are integrated with other actions carried out in other media. In this way, it is important and necessary to observe the relationships established and the potential and actual integrations with other systems and policies, organizations and individuals. It is therefore necessary to take a systemic view of the solution you are developing, where all the influential elements in this system are observed.

It is important to note, from the research carried out, the growing importance that design activity and its practitioner, the designer, have achieved in the context of organizations/companies and contemporary society as a whole, as well as the dynamic movement of their role and competencies within these organizations.

Even though this is a case study, which in itself is already limited in relation to the universe of the designer's work, and in relation to the conclusions it can generate, the statements made by designers and especially non-designers point to a growing appreciation of this professional, as well as an increasing integration of their activity with a growing number of areas of knowledge.

It can be seen that in a complex society, interconnected by a multitude of devices and technologies and made up of infinite variables, which sometimes behaves systemically and sometimes chaotically, designers are called upon to mobilize their multidisciplinary skills and their ability to connect different types of knowledge. In this way, they are placed in key roles in this context, as one of the professionals most adapted and prepared for innovation, a necessity of the new times that contemporary society is experiencing.

Another very clear issue that emerged from this research is that the topic of the designer's role and competencies in multidisciplinary teams is very broad, comprising a significant range of aspects and relationships that need to be studied in depth. This breadth suggests that this field should be revisited in new research and explorations, both qualitative and quantitative, so that we can increasingly understand how design activity and its professionals fit into these collective spaces and organizations, what skills they need to develop in order to perform their job well, and how they relate to other individuals in teams and areas of knowledge in order to help build complex solutions that focus on individuals, clients and users of the solutions.

Mainly on the issues where designers and non-designers showed different points of view, where there was greater controversy, for example on the relationship between design and art (subjectivity and objectivity of the activity), on the interpretation of complex contexts, and on ways to enhance and disseminate the work of the designer and his process within organizations from other fields of knowledge that are beginning to integrate the designer into their staff.

In this way, their unique knowledge and way of thinking and acting can be applied to other areas of the organization, moving away from the more operational and restrictive areas towards more strategic and broad areas, where their potential and skills for approaching and solving problems and generating creative and innovative solutions can be put to good use.

# 7. REFERENCES

ASENDORPF, Jens B. Psychologie der Personlichkeit. Berlin: Springer, 2004.

BAUMAN, Zygmunt. The society of uncertainty. Bologna: Ed.Il Mulino, 1999.

BAUMAN, Z. Modernidade liquida. Rio de Janeiro: Zahar, 2001.

BAUDRILLARD, J. For a Critique of the Political Economy of the Sign. St. Louis: Telos Press, 1972.

BAUDRILLARD, J. La Societé de Consommations. Paris: S.G.P.P. 1970.

BERG, B. L. (1998). Qualitative Research Methods for the Social Sciences. 3ª ed.

MA (USA): Allyn & Bacon. Gil, A. C. (1995). Methods and techniques of social research. 5th ed. Sâo Paulo: Atlas.

BEST. K. Design Management: Managing Design Strategy, Process and Implementation. Lausanne, Switzerland, Published by AVA Publishing SA, 2006.

BODKER, S. Creating Conditions for Participation: Conflicts and Resources in Systems Design, Human Computer Interaction, 1996.

BOMFIM, G. Fundamentos de uma Teoria Transdisciplinar do Design: morfologia dos objetos de uso e sistemas de comunicação. Studies in Design. V V, n. 2. dec 1997.

BORJA DE MOZOTA, B. Design Management: Using Design to Build Brand Value and Corporate Innovation. New York, Allworth Press, 2003.

BRANZI, Andrea. Weak and Diffuse Modernity: The World of Projects at the beginning of the 21st Century. Paris: ed. Skira Architecture Library S., 1996.

BRANZI, Andrea. Modernità debole e difusa: il mondo del progetto all'inizio del XXI secolo. Milano: Ed. Skira, 2006.

BROWN,T. Design Thinking. Harvard Business Review. June, 2008.

http://www.ideo.com/images/uploads/thoughts/IDEO_HBR_Design_Thinking.pdf.

BROWN, Tim. Change by design: how design thinking transforms organizations and inspires innovation. New York: HarperCollins, 2009.

CAMARINHA-MATOS, L., AND AFSARMANESH, H. "A framework for virtual organization creation in a breeding environment", Annual Reviews in Control, 2007.

CAMARINHA-MATOS, L., et al. "Collaborative networked organizations - Concepts and practice in manufacturing enterprises", Computers & Industrial Engineering, 2009.

CANNERI, Diego In MAURI, Francesco. Progettare progettando strategia. Milano: Ed. Dunob, 1996.

CARDOSO D. R. Design, Material Culture and the Fetishism of Objects. Arcos, Rio de Janeiro, v. 1, n. 1, p. 14-39, 1998.

CARDOSO, Rafael. Design for a complex world. Sao Paulo: Cosac Naify, 2013.

CARROL, J. B. Human cognitive abilities: A survey of factor-analytic studies. New York, NY: Cambridge University Press, 1993.

CASTELLS, M. The information age: economy, society, and culture. vol. 1 The rise of the network society. Oxford: Blackwell, 1996.

CASTELLS, Manuel. The network society. Sao Paulo: Paz e Terra, 1999.

CAUTELA, Cabirio. Strumenti di design management. Milan: FrancoAngeli, 2007.

CAUTELA, Cabirio; ZURLO, Francesco. Productive relations: design and strategy in contemporary business. Milano: Aracne, 2006.

CELASHCI, Flaviano and DESERTI, Alessandro. Design e Innovazione: strumenti e pratiche per la ricerca applicata, Milan: Carocci, 2007.

CROSS, N. (ed.) Design Participation: Proceedings of the Design Research Society's Conference 1971, Academy Editions, London, UK, 1972.

CROSS, N., & NATHENSON, M. Design methods and learning methods. In J. Powell and R. Jacques (Eds.), Design Science: Method. Guildford: Westbury House, 1981.

CROSS, N. "Designerly Ways of Knowing." Design Studies 3.4, 1982.

CROSS, Nigel; DORST, Kees; ROOZENBURG, Norbert (Org.). Research in design thinking. Delft: Delft University Press, 1992.

CROSS, N. Discovering design ability. In R. Buchanan and V. Margolin (Eds.), Discovering Design: Explorations in Design Studies. Chicago, IL: The University of Chicago Press, 1995.

CROSS, Nigel. Design Research: A Disciplined Conversation. Design Issues, v. 15, n. 2, p. 5-10, 1999.

CROSS, N.G. EDMONDS E., (eds) Expertise in Design. Creativity and Cognition Studios Press, Sydney, Australia, 2003.

CROSS, N. Design Thinking: Understanding How Designers Think and Work, Berg, Oxford and New York, 2011.

DAMATTA, R. Oficio do Etnòlogo ou como ter Anthropological Blues. In: NUNES, E. (org). The sociological adventure. RJ: Zahar, 1978.

DAMATTA, R. Relativizando: uma introduçao à Antropologia Social, Petrópolis Vozes, 1981.

DELEUZE, G.; GUATTARI, F. Capitalisme et Schizophrénie 2. Mille Plateaux. Paris: Éditions De Minuit, 1980 (Portuguese translation: DELEUZE, G.; GUATTARI, F. Mil platôs: Capitalism and schizophrenia. Vol. I. Sâo Paulo, Ed. 34, 2004).

DE MORAES, D. Metaproject: the design of design. Sâo Paulo: Blucher, 2010.

DESERTI, A. Intorno al progetto: concretizzare l'innovazione. In: CELASCHI, F.; DESERTI, A. Design e innovazione: strumenti e pratiche per la ricerca applicata. Rome: Carocci Editore, 2007.

DORST, K. The problem of Design Problems . In: Design Thinking Research Symposium, Sydney, University of Technology, 2003.

DREYFUS, H., & DREYFUS. S. Mind over machine: The power of human intuition and expertise in the era of the computer. New York: Free Press, 1986.

DREYFUSS, Henry. Designing for People. Allworth Press; illustrated edition, 2003

DREYFUS, H.L. From Socrates to Artificial Intelligence: The Limits of Rule-Based Rationality. Unpublished lecture notes of the first 2003 Spinoza Lecture at the University of Amsterdam, 2003.

DREYFUS H.L. Can there be a better source of meaning than every day practices? Unpublished lecture notes of the second 2003 Spinoza Lecture at the University of Amsterdam, 2003.

FRASCARA, J. "Graphic Design: Fine Art or Social Science?" in The Idea of Design: A Design Issues Reader, edited by Victor Margolin and Richard Buchanan, pp. 4455, Cambridge: MIT Press, 1995.

. Diseno Gràfico para la gente: Comunicaciones de masa y cambio social. Buenos Aires: Ediciones Infinito, 2000.

FRIEDMAN, K. "Creating design knowledge: from research into practice" in E W L Norman and P H Roberts (eds.), Design and Technology Educational Research and Development:

The Emerging International Research Agenda, Department of Design and Technology, Loughborough University, Loughborough (2001).

Theory construction in design research: criteria: approaches, and methods. Design Studies, 24, 2003.

GILL, P.; STEWART, K.; TREASURE E.; CHADWICK, B. Methods of data collection in qualitative research: interviews and focus groups. In: British Dental Journal, v. 204, 2008, p.291-295.

GIOVINAZZO, R. A. (200i). Focus Group in Qualitative Research - Fundamentals and Reflections. Administraçâo On-Line - Pràtica - Pesquisa - Ensino, 2, n° 4.

GODOI, C. K,; MATTOS, P. L. C. L.. Qualitative interview: research tool and dialogic event. In: SILVA, A. B.; GODOI, C. K.; BANDEIRA-DE-MELO, R. (eds). Qualitative research in organizational studies: paradigms, strategies and methods. 2. ed. Sao Paulo, 2010, p. 301-323.

GONZÀLES REY, F. L. (2002). Qualitative Research in Psychology - Paths and Challenges. Sao Paulo: Pioneira Thomson Learning. Morgan, D. L. (1997). Focus Groups as Qualitative Research. London: SAGE Publications.

GOUVEIA, L. The Concept of the Digital Network in the Face of Social Media. XI Forum "Communiquer etEntreprendre". 26/27 November. RCMFM and Fernando Pessoa University. Porto, Portugal, 2009.

KRIPPENDORFF, K. The semantic turn. A new foundation for design. Boca-Raton: Taylor & Francis, 2006.

KRIPPENDORFF, K. Metodologia de anàlisis de contenido: teoria e pràctica. Barcelona, Ediciones Paidós, 1990.

LATOUR, B. Science in Action: How to follow scientists and engineers in society. Sao Paulo: UNESP, 2000.

LAWSON, B. How Designers Think, London: The Architectural Press, 1980.

LEVITT, Theodore. The imagination of marketing. Translated by Auriphero Berrance Simoes. 2ª ed. Sao Paulo: Editora Atlas, 1990.

LÉVY, Pierre. Opening up semantic space in favor of collective intelligence. Magazine

Eletrônica de Comunicaçâo Informaçâo & Inovaçâo em Saù. Rio de Janeiro, v.1, n.1, p.129-140, jan.-jun., 2007.

______. Collective intelligence: towards an anthropology of cyberspace. 4.ed. Sâo Paulo: Loyola, 2003.

______. Cyberculture. 2.ed. Sâo Paulo: Editora 34, 2000.

______. What is virtual? Sâo Paulo: Editora 34, 1996.

LOWGREN, J., & STOLTERMAN, E. - Design of information technology-material without qualitites * Lund: Studentlitteratur, 1998.

LOWGREN, J., & STOLTERMAN, E. Thoughtful interaction design: A design perspective on information technology. Cambridge, MA: MIT Press, 2004.

LOCKWOOD, T. Design Thinking: integrating innovation, customer experience, and brand value. Edited by Thomas Lockwood.-3rd ed. 2009.

MALDONADO, Tomàs. The Future of Modernity. Milano: Feltrinelli, 1987.

MALDONADO, T. Disegno Industriale: un riesame. Milano: G. Feltrinelli, 1999.

MALINOWSKI B. A scientific theory of culture. Sao Paulo: Zahar; 1975.

MANZINI, Ezio; JÉGOU, François. Scenery design. In: BERTOLA, Paola;

MANZINI, Ezio (Org.) Design multiverso: appunti di fenomenologia del design. Milan: Edizioni POLI.design, 2004.

MANZINI, Ezio; VEZZOLI, Carlo. The development of sustainable products. Sao Paulo: University Press, 2002.

MANZINI, E.; VEZZOLI, C. A strategic design approach to develop sustainable product service systems: examples taken from the 'environmentally friendly innovation' Italian prize. Journal of Cleaner Production. v. 11, p. 851-857, 2003.

MANZINI, E., VEZZOLI, C. Product-service systems and sustainability. Opportunities for sustainable solutions. Paris: UNEP Publisher, 2002.

MANZINI, E.; VEZZOLI, C. Lo sviluppo di prodotti sostenibili. Milano: Maggioli Editore, 1998.

MAURI, Francesco. Progettare Progettando Strategia. Milan: Ed. Dunob, 1996.

MERONI, A. Strategic design: where are we now? Reflection around the foundations of a recent discipline. In: STRATEGIC DESIGN RESEARCH JOURNAL, Vol.1:31-38 July-December 2008. Unisinos.

MEYER, G. C. Reflections on the characterization of scientific research and professional practice in design. In: Brazilian Congress of Research and Development in Design, Sao Paulo, 2008a.

. Different perspectives on the study of emotions: comments from Ergonomics and Psychology. In: Brazilian Congress of Research and Development in Design, Sao Paulo, 2008b.

MOGGRIDGE, B. Design Interactions. Cambridge, MA: MIT Press, 2007.

MONT, O. Product-Service Systems. Stockholm, Swedish EPA, AFR-report 288:83, 2000.

MONT, O. K.; Clarifying the concept of product-service system. Journal of Cleaner

Production, v. 10, p. 237-245, 2002. Revista Produçao Online, v.10, n.4, p. 837-860, dez., 2010.

MORAES, R. Content Analysis: limits and possibilities. In: ENGERS, M.E.A. (Org). Paradigms and methodologies of research in education. Porto Alegre, EDIPUCRS, 1994.

MONT, O.; LINDHQVIST, T. The role of public policy in advancement of productservice system. Journal of Cleaner Production. v. 11, p. 905 - 914, 2003.

MORELLI, N. Product-service system, a perspective shift for designers: a case study in a design of a telecentre. Design Studies. v. 24, p. 73 - 99, 2003.

MORIN, Edgar. The need for complex thinking. In: MENDES, Cândido (Org.); LARRETA, Enrique (Ed.). Representation and complexity. Rio de Janeiro: Garamond, 2003, p. 69-78. Available at: http://unesdoc.unesco.org/images/0013/001317/131796por.pdf> Accessed on: June 9, 2012.

Science with a conscience. 14ª ed. Rio de Janeiro: Bertrand Brasil, 2010.

Introduction to complex thinking. 4th ed. Porto Alegre: Sulina, 2011.

MOSCOVICI, Fela. Interpersonal development: group training - Rio de Janeiro: José Olympio, 2002.

NORMAN, Donald A. Cognitive Engineering. In: Norman, Donald A.; Draper, Stephen (eds.) User Centered System Design: new perspectives on human-computer interaction. Hillsdale: Lawrence Erlbaum, 1986. p. 31-61.

NORMAN, Donald A. O design do dia-a-dia. Rio de Janeiro: Rocco, 2006.

ONO, Maristela. Design and culture: essential harmony. Curitiba: Author's edition, 2006.

PARKER, G. M. The Power of Teams: a practical guide to implementing high-performance cross-functional teams. Rio de Janeiro: Campus, 1995.

PRAHALAD, C.K. & RAMASWAMY, V. Co-creation Experiences: The Nest Practice in Value Creation. Journal of Interactive Marketing, 18(3), 5-14, 2004.

SANDERS, Elizabeth B.N.; STAPPERS, Pieter Jan. Co-creation and the new landscapes of design. Delft: Taylor & Francis Group, Codesign Journal, Vol. 4, No. 1, March 2008, p 5-18, 2008.

SCHEIN, E. H. (1984) Coming to a new Awareness of Organizational Culture. Sloan management Review Winter - Massachusetts Institute of Technology.

SCHEIN, E. H. Guia de sobrevivência da Cultura Corporativa.Rio de Janeiro: José Olympio, 2001.

SCHEIN, E. H. Three cultures of management:the key to organizational learning. Sloan Management Review, Boston: Fall, 1996SCHON, D., A. The Reflective Practitioner: How Professionals Think in Action. New York, Basic Books, 1983.

SIMON, H., A. The Sciences of the artificial, 3rd Ed. Cambridge, MA: MIT Press (1969/2001).

STOMPFF, Guido in: Facilitating Team Cognition - How Designers mirror what NPD Teams Do. Ed 2012.

VERGANTI, R. Innovating Through Design. Harvard Business Review. December, p.114-122, 2006.

WHYTE, W. F. Sociedade de Esquina. Rio de Janeiro, Jorge Zahar, 2005.

WINOGRAD, T. From Computing Machinery to Interaction Design, in Beyond Calculation: the Next Fifty Years of Computing, P. Denning and R. Metcalfe (eds), Amsterdam: Springer-Verlag 1997, p. 149-162.

# ANNEX A - TERM OF AUTHORIZATION TO CARRY OUT THE RESEARCH AT PROCERGS RS

# ANNEX B - FOCUS GROUP APPLICATION GUIDE APPLIED TO THE DESIGNERS OF THE COMPANY STUDIED.

Below is the focus group application guide drawn up for this research, with its main questions, sub-items and the time allotted for each topic:

| Questions | Time |
| --- | --- |
| **1 - Introduction**<br>Good morning, my name is Ubiratan Silva and I'm here as a researcher doing an experiment that will be analyzed in a master's thesis I'm developing at UNISINOS on design. First of all, I'd like to thank you for your willingness to take part in this experiment. This is of fundamental importance to the research. But before I start the discussion, I need to give you some information so that you feel completely comfortable giving your opinion on the topic of the focus group and the questions that will revolve around this topic. | 5' |
| **2 - Presentation of the research objectives General**<br>- Reflect on the role and competencies of the designer in multidisciplinary teams.<br>**Specifics:**<br>- Identify expectations that designers have about their role and skills of the designer working in teams.<br>- To identify expectations of NON-designers who are part of teams with designers about the role and competencies of the designer.<br>- To establish a parallel between the expectations of designers and non-designers about the role and competencies of the designer in the context studied. - Identify aspects related to the nature (type) of the transformation of the designer's role in an organization/company and in teams.<br>- Identify factors that influence the role of the designer in organizations/companies.<br>- Identify the difficulties faced by designers in carrying out their professional activity in multidisciplinary teams. | 5' |
| **Information about the focus group**<br>First of all, I would like to ask you to make yourselves very comfortable, your names and identities will not be revealed in the research, and you will be able to access the content before publication. The company has legally authorized | 5' |

| | |
|---|---|
| the study and I have here with me a consent form to use the content of the interview for scientific research. Secondly, the interview will be recorded on audio with a cell phone voice recorder, and on video using a camera that will be installed in a corner of the room. This will be done because I will later need to transcribe it and use the technique of content analysis in the research to gain a deeper understanding of what you said and how you said it, so if you don't mind, it will be recorded, okay? Finally, I'd like to make it clear that this is a scientific experiment, so I'm here as a researcher and although it's difficult, I'm going to ask you to see me as a researcher, someone from the outside, who knows nothing about this context, okay? Another similar research technique will be applied to other people | |
| non-designers in the company in order to compare the different views on the same subject, the role and skills of the designer in multidisciplinary teams. | |
| **On the dynamics of the focus group** The dynamics of the focus group will be like this: I'll ask you a question and you'll answer, I may ask you to expand on the answer if I haven't understood something, the questions are very open and broad. Sometimes it may seem that the questions are similar, but that's just so that we can delve deeper into the subject through different paths and visions and see the issue from different angles. We have the room reserved for two hours and during that time you can interrupt each other to talk, remember cases, situations if you want, tell us about a particular case to illustrate, the most important thing here is that everyone is spontaneous and can give their opinion on what is going to be asked, which is very simple and deals with our own reality. All clear, any questions? Everyone feel free... can we get started? Here we go. | 5' |
| **1 - Motivations of the Designer** (broader, more familiar issue) The first question is to talk about the motivations that led to your interest in the design profession. **1.1 - How did you become interested in the design profession?** | 15' |
| **2 - The Designer's Role and Skills** Let's talk a bit about what you think about a professional activity that particularly interests us here, design, and what the role of this professional (designer) would be and what skills are needed to perform this function. **2.2 - What do you think a person needs to have or know in order to work as a designer?** | 25' |

| | |
|---|---|
| 2.2.1 - What other professions would you compare to design (in terms of skills, methods (way of working, process and relationships) why? <br> 2.2.2 - What other professions do you consider distinct or different from design (in terms of skills, methods (way of working, process and relationships) why? <br> 2.2.3 - What do you see as the role of the designer in general? <br> 2.2.4 - What do you see as the role of the designer at PROCERGS? <br> 2.2.5 - During your work process at PROCERGS, which competencies do you involve/use? <br> 2.2.6 - Within the PROCERGS context, do you think that the role of the designer is static and tends to remain the same, or is it mutable and tends to change within the organization? | |
| **3 - Designer Working in Teams** <br> We need to know what you think about working in teams, which is a common practice here at the company. <br> **3.1 - Do you think designers work better alone or as part of a team? Why is that?** <br> 3.1.1 - What personal characteristics do you think are important for teamwork? <br> 3.1.2 - What problems do designers face when working in teams? and at PROCERGS? <br> 3.1.3 - What are the advantages of designers working in teams? And at PROCERGS? <br> 3.1.4 - What tasks do you think a designer should take care of at PROCERGS? <br> 3.1.5 - And which tasks should he NOT take on? | 15' |
| **4 - The Designer's Purpose and Contribution** <br> Tell us a bit about what he does (what would be the result of his work). <br> **4.1 - What do you see as the main purpose and objective of a designer as a professional?** <br> 4.1.1 - What does the designer offer people? For example: values, sensations, feelings, meaning, illusion, truth, good taste, pride, elegance, sophistication, etc? <br> 4.1.2 - What can designers NOT guarantee from their work? What is outside their remit? | 15' |
| **5 - Designer image** <br> **5.1 - If you were to describe a designer to someone who had never heard of them, how would you describe them? Explain.** <br> 5.1.1 - What kind of professional is a designer? <br> 5.1.2 - How would you describe the day-to-day life of a designer? | 15' |

| | |
|---|---|
| 5.1.3 - How is PROCERGS different?<br>5.1.4 - Do you think that choosing design as a profession would be a good choice for your children (if you have any)? Would you recommend the profession to a relative who has not yet chosen their field?<br>5.1.5 - How important do you think it is? | |
| **6 - Organizational Culture**<br>This research also seeks to understand how organizational culture influences the role of the designer. Organizational culture is understood here as the set of habits, practices, methods, rules and formal and informal agreements that characterize an organization. So the question is as follows:<br>**6.1 - How do you think the company's organizational culture influences the role of the designer?** | **15'** |
| Finalizing<br>Would anyone like to comment on any outstanding points? Are there any other points to be made? I would like to thank you for your attention and for taking the time to discuss this and to inform you that when the research is completed, a new meeting will be scheduled with the participant group to present and discuss the results of the research and possible applications of these results in the search for improvement and expansion of the role of the designer within the organization. Thank you. | **5'** |
| **Total Estimated Time** | **120'** |
| **Total Time Taken** | **110'** |
| With each question, the mediator/researcher always sought to deepen the answers with the following questions: **explain this better, I don't understand, could you give me examples? cite a situation? exemplify** | |

# ANNEX C - IN-DEPTH INTERVIEW GUIDE Semi-structured interviews with non-designers

| Interview script with non-designers | |
| --- | --- |
| **Questions** | **Time** |
| **Presentation**<br><br>Good morning, my name is Ubiratan silva and I'm here as a researcher doing an experiment that will be analyzed in a master's thesis I'm developing at UNISINOS on design. First of all, I'd like to thank you for your willingness to take part, as this conversation is of fundamental importance to the research, and before I start I'd like to give you some information so that you feel completely at ease giving your opinion on the subject of the interview. | 3' |
| **Information about the interview**<br><br>First of all, I would like to ask you to make yourself very comfortable, names and identities will not be revealed in the research, you will be able to access the content before publication, the company has legally authorized the study and I have here a consent form to use the content of the interview for scientific analysis.<br><br>Secondly, the interview will be recorded on audio with a cell phone voice recorder, because later I will need to transcribe it and use the content analysis technique in the research, so if you don't mind, it will be recorded, okay?<br><br>Lastly, this is a scientific experiment, so I'm here as a researcher and although it's difficult, I'm going to ask you to see me as a researcher, an outsider, who knows nothing about this context, okay? This same interview will be applied to other non-designers in the company. | 3' |
| **On the dynamics of the interview**<br><br>The dynamics of the interview will be like this: I'll ask you a question and you'll answer it, and I may ask you to expand on it if you don't understand something about the answer. Sometimes it may seem that the questions are similar, but this is just so that you can delve deeper into the subject and see the issue from different angles.<br><br>We have the room booked for an hour, although the interview should last a maximum of 30 to 40 minutes and during this time you can interrupt me to talk, remember cases, situations if you want, tell me a case to illustrate, the most important thing here is that you are spontaneous and can give your opinion on what is going to be asked, which is quite simple. | 3' |

| | |
|---|---|
| All clear, any questions? feel free... can we get started? come on... | |
| **Identification of the interviewee**<br>First of all, I'd like to ask you to introduce yourself briefly with your name, position, length of time in the company and academic qualifications.<br>**1 - Importance of the Designer**<br>1.1 - How important is a designer to you? | 5' |
| **2 - Role and competencies**<br>2.1 - What do you think a person needs to have in order to work as a designer? and to work as a designer at PROCERGS?<br>2.1    - What other professions would you compare to design (in terms of skills, methods (way of working, process and relationships) why?<br>2.2    - What other professions would you NOT compare to design (in terms of skills, methods (way of working, process and relationships) why?<br>2.3    - What do you see as the role of the designer in general?<br>2.4    - And what would the role of the designer be at PROCERGS?<br>2.5    - Within the PROCERGS context, do you think the role of the designer is static and tends to remain the same, or is it mutable and tends to change within the organization? | 10' |
| **3 - Teams**<br>3.1    - Do you think designers work better alone or as part of a team? Why is that?<br>3.2    - What personal characteristics do you think are important for working in teams?<br>3.3    - What problems do you face working with designers in teams? and at PROCERGS?<br>3.4    - What are the advantages of working with designers in teams? And at PROCERGS?<br>3.5    - In the solutions developed at PROCERGS, what tasks do you think the designer should take care of? And which tasks should they NOT take care of? | 5' |
| **4 - Image**<br>4.1 - If you were to describe a designer to someone who had never heard of them, how would you describe them?<br>4.2 - What image do you have of a professional designer? Explain. You can talk about physical aspects, psychological aspects, etc., to understand what image you have of a designer. | 5' |
| **5 - Organizational Culture**<br>5.1 - Do you think that the company's organizational culture influences the | 3' |

| role of the designer? in what way? | |
| --- | --- |
| **Estimated time** | 37'<br>(on average) |
| **Real Time** | It varied between 25 and 40 minutes. |

# ANNEX D - MODEL CONSENT FORM FOR PARTICIPATION IN FOCUS GROUPS AND IN-DEPTH INTERVIEWS

Me   ,

ID: PROCERGS employee

I agree to participate, as a volunteer, in the study which has as its responsible researcher the Master's student in Design at UNISINOS **Ubiratan Silva da Silva,** who can be contacted by e-mail at **ubiratan.s.silva@gmail.com and by telephone at (51)** 93537025. I am aware that the study aims to carry out interviews with employees of the PROCERGS company, with a view, on the part of the aforementioned student, to carrying out research and a master's thesis on the role and competencies of the designer. My participation will consist of giving an interview which will be recorded and transcribed. I understand that this study is for academic research purposes, that the data obtained will not be divulged except with prior authorization, and that in this case the anonymity of the participants will be preserved, thus ensuring my privacy. The student will provide a copy of the interview transcript for my information. Furthermore, I know that I can withdraw from the research at any time and that I will not receive any payment for my participation.

Signature

Porto Alegre, September 8, 2014.

Printed by Books on Demand GmbH, Norderstedt / Germany